T0146792

"Creating Your Leadership Discipline"

JOE CLEGGETT

authorHOUSE®

AuthorHouse™
1663 Liberty Drive
Bloomington, IN 47403
www.authorhouse.com
Phone: 1 (800) 839-8640

Published by AuthorHouse   02/11/2016

ISBN: 978-1-5049-7805-7 (sc)
ISBN: 978-1-5049-7803-3 (hc)
ISBN: 978-1-5049-7804-0 (e)

Library of Congress Control Number: 2016902126

Dedication

This is the easiest decision I have had to make in writing this book. The book is dedicated to my wife Kathy. I met her when I was sixteen years old and she has enriched my life in many ways ever since. She encouraged me to write the book, was always there to help when I needed it, and served as the executive editor throughout. She also gave me my wonderful daughter Erin, our first author, who has written three books of her own. Also, Erin and our son-in-law Sean, gave us Gavin and Evelyn, our two grandchildren, who are the center of our life and help keep us positive and young. They also have two dogs, Simon and Izzy who take me for walks most days and help to keep me healthy and happy. Thank you all.

Contents

Acknowledgments

The many people I have had the pleasure to know throughout my life should all be acknowledged for their ideas that have led to the contents of this book. Certainly, my extended family needs to be mentioned and thanked for all they have done and continue to do to make my life as good as it is. Many of the people I have worked with over the years have also contributed a lot to my success and the writing of this book. Without them I would have never been a leader at all and certainly not able to write a book on how to help others **Create a Leadership Discipline** for themselves. On an historical note, I really want to acknowledge the men and women who founded and kept the United States as a free society. **Life, Liberty and the Pursuit of Happiness** remain the basis of our society and being brought up in the **cradle of liberty** gave me the ability to achieve and use my imagination to develop better solutions to the problems we meet every day in leading others. It is true that **"you get the most out of people when they are happy and not afraid",** and that is what all the work of our founding fathers and those who have preserved this great country have given me. I get up every day and can use my creativity, curiosity, ambition and imagination as a sense of adventure to go about my day, and for that I am most thankful. I am also most grateful that being brought up in a free society has provided me with the emotional talents and sensitivity to honestly believe that ***all lives matter***.

THANK YOU ALL

Prologue

Throughout this book 'talents' will be discussed in a number of ways, including; knowledge, skills, strengths, consciousness, and 'radar' the awareness of others. Understanding these various forms of talents, and recognizing our shortcomings, will help us to create our discipline for leadership. A recent book makes a point, very well, that will help to drive home the point that talents are the basic ingredients of Leadership. This book published in 2008 also provides a good understanding of our changing world. "The Post American World" by Fareed Zakaria provides some insight into what the author describes as the "rise of the rest" instead of the "decline of America". In this book, Zakaria "draws on lessons from the two great power shifts of the past five hundred years—the rise of the Western world and the rise of the United States—to tell us what we can expect from the third shift, 'the rise of the rest",[1] or 'a post American world'. In the chapter of the book entitled "American Power", Zakaria proclaims that "Higher education is America's best industry".[2] In discussing why he believes this he gets into a discussion on the differences in how Americans learn to think as opposed to how Asians and Chinese learn to think. The quote that really drives home the importance of talents is attributed to Tharman Shanmugaratnam, a former minister of education in Singapore, who, after studying the differences in education between his country's system and America's stated "We both have meritocracies---Yours is a 'talent' meritocracy, ours is an exam meritocracy. We know how to train people to take exams; you know how to use people's 'talents' to the fullest. Both are important, but there are some parts of the intellect that we are not able to test well— like creativity, curiosity, a sense of adventure, and ambition. Most of all America has a culture of learning that challenges conventional wisdom, even if it means challenging authority…"[3] As we go through this book it will become clear how important the discussion of these talents are in the development of a leadership discipline and how this quote really sums up this basic ingredient of learning what we do best and using that in leading other people effectively, and most importantly, passionately. Knowing how 'to use people's talents to the fullest' is a great advantage to developing leaders and is enhanced by America's keystone, 'liberty'. Having the ability to learn in a free society is one of the basic ingredients of developing talents. Many leaders believe that freedom, responsibility, integrity, and the ability to attract, develop, and keep talented employees are the keys to success. This book is intended as a roadmap for you to use to develop a successful Leadership Discipline for both your work and your life.

Some would say there are as many definitions of leadership as there are leaders. Most leaders have their own style that has been personalized to their situation and have elements that reflect their own personality, communication style, and priorities. Some leadership positions deal with directing people while others have very little to do with directing people. In most industries interfacing with people is a very important ingredient of leadership. Leaders are constantly directing the efforts of others, explaining situations to clients and justifying costs and decisions to executive management. Today's leader is expected to be an expert in many areas such as finance, statistics, resource allocation, service delivery and marketing. Additionally we want our leaders to be competent in writing, speaking, listening, negotiating, and influencing. All of this required in a world that continues to move faster and faster with every new social media gimmick, and is now dealing with 'the rising of the rest'. It used to be that in the US, a reasonably well-educated individual with good experience in a particular business would make a good leader in that particular industry. Now that has all changed and along with "the rising of the rest" we in America find ourselves in a position of not being the 'automatic' leader of the world's problems and solutions. The growth of our economy is no longer stable and assured. We now have to compete with China, the EU and the others. Although the US is still a driver in the world economy, other countries are also drivers and we have to be able to compete in this new environment. Today's leaders not only need to be well educated and experienced in his/her particular field, they need to be able to act in a proficient way to keep their edge in the world. As Warren Buffet says, "there is no finish line." Leaders need to constantly improve their strengths, principles, and skills needed to deal with people in a conscious manner.

It has been seven years since "The Post American World" was published and much of what was said in that book is well underway in the changes we should expect in how the world operates. Leadership in this new world has to change as well, and what we thought were the right ingredients are no longer sufficient. Many think the new leader needs to be proficient in 'Emotional Intelligence'

EQ as well as the standard old IQ. "Emotional intelligence is the ability to sense, understand, and effectively apply the power and acumen of emotions as a source of human energy, information, connection and influence."[4] *The ability to act intuitively or through 'gut' feelings, with the proper education and experience is the distinguishing talent of the new leader. This ability is not only useful in the business world, but provides a leadership discipline for life. Honestly understanding one's talents, both intuitive (gut) and reasoning (effortful and slower) allows good decisions to be made in a proficient manner, and that is the definition of a good Leadership Discipline.*

Chapter 1
THE SHORTCUT

The first thing you have to know about this book is that I like to tell *stories*. Most of them are *'probably'* true, although on occasion the vivid imagination of my childhood may alter some of the facts. But I assure you this will be of no detriment to what you may learn from reading this book. When telling stories, it is sometimes important to be repetitious in what is being said, so you may read the same point two, three, or even four times in different parts of the book. This lets me drive home an important point about how to discover your *talents* and to create *discipline* to promote what you do best. I hope you enjoy reading the book as much as I enjoyed writing it and I hope my stories help you to know and understand yourself and what you can get out of this book.

The first and probably the most important story is appropriately called *"The Shortcut"*. It takes place when I was about five years old and is about how I got to school as a kid. I am the youngest of five children; my next older sibling is Bill who plays a key part in this story as he also did in many stories throughout my life.

We lived about a mile from the Monatiquot School and the route to the school, although on back roads, was up and over a pretty high hill. My mother would pack me up in the morning in my hand-me-down clothes and give me my lunch in a paper bag and send me off with my personal escort and guardian Bill. We would usually meet up with the notorious Smith boys, Peter was Bills age and Paul was a year older than me. As has been the case throughout my life, I was the youngest and always last in whatever we did. Bill and I would leave the house and the trek would begin. Bill would always be about fifty feet ahead of me and would constantly yell "hurry up, or we'll be late". That mattered to him because he was in the sixth grade, very popular, and wanted to make his mark at the beginning of each day with his friends to assure himself of his stature in the school. I on the other hand was in kindergarten, had a nickname of 'Butchie' and was only interested in blending in and being Billy's brother. We would usually meet up with the Smith boys and the trek would continue. Bill and Peter would lead the parade with Paul somewhere in the middle and Butchie picking up the rear. It would all go pretty well except for the constant bullying I had to put up with from Paul, who was a large (fat) kid who always had to be poking or prodding someone smaller than him. Occasionally the command would come from the top, Bill or Peter, "leave him alone". If it came from Bill it would usually include "or I'll kick your ass". This would stop any problem with Paul, as any one knew that if Bill said he would 'kick your ass', he would.

About ten minutes into the trek we would be entering the Thayer Academy woods which would be the first *'shortcut'* in the journey and that was pretty nice. We would walk on paths cut through the woods covered with years of pine needles that had dropped off the 'gigantic' (about 30 feet high) pine trees to the athletic fields of Thayer Academy.

Thayer Academy, by the way, is a really good private school started by General Sylvanus Thayer as a prep school for West Point. It also had a middle school called Thayer Lands for younger children. When we crossed the athletic fields we would cross a street and enter through the gate into the stone-walled, forbidden property of Thayer Lands, hurriedly make our way through the playground to the ***'Berlin Wall'*** that we would have to climb over as there was no exit gate. Once again the order would come from the top "hurry up Butch or we'll get caught" as no one was allowed to go through Thayer Lands and climb the stone wall to escape and take the ***'shortcut'*** to Monatiquot. Monatiquot, by the way, is an old Indian name ***probably*** from the Wampanoag Tribe that inhabited the area before the arrival of settlers from Europe. We would be told by the teachers at Monatiquot every so often "not to go through Thayer Lands, you must go around and down Academy Street". No 'shortcuts'. And now the crux of the story; ***'the wall'***.

Bill, Peter, and Paul were like monkeys, up one side, stand on the top, and then down the other side onto the grass sidewalk. I, on the other hand, would stand and look at the wall and wish it wasn't there as I hated to climb that tremendously high wall, roll myself over the top (no standing for me) and slide down the other side hoping to find a protruding stone to catch my foot before dropping to the grass. Every day was the same; I never got used to climbing the wall, but I liked the ***'shortcut'*** because that was how we got to school and it saved a lot of time. I never got hurt, but was always a bit scared that I would because of the height of the wall. I don't think I ever walked all the way up the hill and down Academy Street to get to school, it just didn't make any sense and took a lot more time.

When you can accomplish your goal without hurting anyone, (especially yourself) except those who want to make it harder for no good reason, take the *'shortcut'*, even if it may be a little scary. That is what this chapter and book is all about.

You can read all the books I have read to find out what your **talents** are and how to create a **discipline** to use them advantageously or you can read this chapter and book to save a lot of time by taking the *'shortcut'*. It will take a lot of time to learn what your **talents** are and how to use them productively and having a good start on what to look for in the reading material will help and hopefully make it fun. Oh, and by the way, the *'Berlin Wall'* at Thayer Lands was about five feet high. Unfortunately for me, I was about thirty inches high at five years old, and yes, my good friends still call me 'Butch'. Climbing that wall every day also helped me create a discipline and build my confidence.

You may also be interested to know that the Monatiquot School and the Monatiquot River are located in the town of Braintree, which was incorporated in 1640 as one of the first towns in America. Both John Adams and John Hancock were born in Braintree. The history of the area, as part of the **cradle of liberty,** was a part of my upbringing, always being told of **the importance of individual freedoms and to respect that same freedom in others**. You will see that this attitude and **unconditional respect for all will carry throughout the book.**

Now let's get on with Chapter 1 and *'Your Shortcut'*.

Adding Value to a Changing World

The world is changing in many ways and at a staggering rate that affects business, political, and social decisions. The truth will change rapidly with information provided by the latest social media gimmick and our new leaders will be forced to direct people, and themselves, through the maze of information created by what is popular at any specific moment in time. The United States will no longer be the automatic leader in many instances, and working to maintain our leadership will become more and more challenging. There are also changes in leadership in which the leader of tomorrow doesn't look like the leader of yesterday. One key change here is that the new leadership is more focused on *'teams'* and not just individual leaders. This change is one of the reasons to focus on a *'Leadership Discipline'* for life as well as one for the particular position you may have in business. Look around at how things happen in todays society, be it social or work related, there is a need for leadership at every level of life. There will be a lot more on this later, but it is important to begin by knowing how important *individual leadership* is in our democracy, and how important it is to have *people who want to lead, take responsibility, and add value to their position in life.*

The idea for this book was never to help create the next Winston Churchill, Hillary Clinton, Bill Gates, or Mary Barra. And for those sports enthusiasts, the discussions on *talents* are not intended to compare the readers *talents* to those of Tiger Woods or Serena Williams.

Certainly, all those mentioned have attained a place among the great leaders of our society, but the real leaders of the world are those who get up every day and lead themselves and others in an effort to make it a better place to live and prosper. *This book is intended to help those who have a passion for successfully leading themselves and other people in their everyday work and life.* Leadership requirements are going to change just as the world is changing and we will continue to create our heroes of business in flashy CEOs and our sports legends in the best tennis player and golfer, but any real change in the value of everyday life will come from the leaders who continue to get up and, without all the hype, lead people in their daily struggle of life, at work and at home. These leaders will have to know their **talents** and the **talents** of those they lead to successfully make a positive difference. They will have to master the art of being *'conscious'* of themselves and others, being aware of their *"inner and outer worlds"* [1] and be able to accept the perceptions of those they may not even like. Always remember that "we are social beings, hardwired from our evolutionary past to **equate relationships with survival.** We want to work with other people in solving problems, **tell them stories and hear stories from them**, create new ideas with them because if we didn't do those things on the savannah 100,000 years ago, we died." [2] All people need to have a purpose and to **add value to life.**

We in the US still have some great advantages to help our people become leaders and add value to life. Our education system is still the best in the world. Opportunity remains strong in business, medicine, social services and other industries due to the experiences gained in our 250 years as a free society. *"Life, Liberty, and the Pursuit of Happiness"* remain the basis of our society. Being brought up with these beliefs gives us the ability to achieve and use our imagination in developing better solutions to the problems we meet every day regardless of how the world may change. Maybe Carl Reiner said it best in his statement *"You get the best out of people when they are happy and not afraid"*, and that's what we in America have the privilege to be.

Another reason for my writing this book is to try to give the reader an understanding of what is necessary to create a **leadership discipline** for the business world and for life in general, considering the world we live in today. It is also to share my twenty-five years of leadership experience and work in developing my own leadership discipline, that serves me well both in business and life. Although more challenged today, the US still has a leading position and many benefits that our new leaders need to take advantage of, especially in education and experience. It certainly is true that the US is experiencing *'the rising of the rest'*, but it is also true America is far from any *'decline'* in our ability to lead. The rules are certainly changing, and the **talents** of the people in the US will continue to be the fundamental ingredients of our new leaders. "The evidence is clear that the most effective groups are those who possess **human abilities**, empathy above all, social sensitivity, storytelling, collaborating, solving problems together and building relationships," [3] all of which are part of our upbringing in our *free society*.

The first idea for writing this book occurred to me after completing two one year long mentoring programs I developed for twelve managers ready to make the *'leap'* to leadership, remembering that *good managers do things right, and good leaders do the right thing.'* Working as the mentor with these twelve talented young engineering managers made me realize how many truly talented young people we have who may never get the chance to lead others because they have not created a **discipline** for themselves to promote their **talents** and demonstrate their **values**. Of the twelve mentees, ten went on to leadership positions and hopefully the mentoring helped them to demonstrate their **value as leaders**.

"Creating a Leadership Discipline" was originally written and given by me as a six part presentation to fifty or so managers in a management seminar developed to encourage managers to passionately engage in the mission of the Florida Turnpike. The management seminar also included other lecturers whose topics concentrated on improving one's self and learning to manage and lead others effectively in the operation of the Turnpike. Working with this group of professional educators and front line managers encouraged me even more to find a way to help

people learn how to use their **talents** in leading others. In the years that have passed since the mentoring programs and the lectures to the Turnpike managers, it has become even clearer to me that people who want to succeed have to have a well thought out **life discipline** that is heavily focused on those **talents** and **social skills** necessary to work and interact with others effectively.

Having been an executive in some large engineering firms I was very lucky in my career to be able to develop my leadership skills and create a **work discipline** for the particular units that I managed. Being a mentor to some younger managers helped me to understand how the leadership role is changing considering all that is happening in the world, and how that is affecting the US business advantage. The management seminar for the Florida Turnpike drove home the point to me that to be a good leader, you really have to be involved passionately and consciously in what you are doing, especially if you are going to lead others.

There is no doubting that the US may lead in fewer instances and that the competition is going to get tougher for the next generation of leaders. We still have the advantage of great education and our *"talent meritocracy"* which gives us *"creativity, curiosity, a sense of adventure, and ambition"*. We have always been the most productive working people in the world because we **think harder and work smarter**. In addition to all our education, experience, and hard work, we also have the benefit of being brought up in a *'free society'* that provides us with that *"creativity, curiosity, a sense of adventure and ambition"* that is so helpful in the development of **emotional EQ talents** and interpersonal skills that are the heart and soul of understanding and leading others. Other countries may be able to match our educational and experience talents, but few, if any, can match the **respect we develop for people in general** through our upbringing in our free society. There is a good quote from "Executive EQ" that says it better than me. ***"No the heart isn't just a pump, as cardiologists describe it. It is more. Scientists can measure its energy from five feet away. It radiates. It activates our deepest values, transforming them from something we think about to something we live. It knows things our mind does not, cannot. The heart is the place of courage and spirit, integrity and commitment. It is a source of energy and deep feelings that calls us to learn, cooperate, lead, and serve."*** [4]

When I first started studying leadership and talents, I did not have the knowledge or respect of the emotional aspects in understanding and leading people. As I have progressed in my knowledge of the subject, it has become clear to me how important *emotional talents* are in leading people and how being brought up in the US has provided me with such an advantage in this area. Most of our *talents* or *strengths* contain some form of emotional intelligence. If you learn nothing else in this book, make sure you know how important it is to *"acknowledge and value feelings"*, [5] yours and those of others. That in itself is truly the differentiator for those from a *free society* in leading others in life.

I have always had really good people around me, have worked for some of the best companies in the world, and have been able to continue learning through education and experience. These advantages remain today for our new leaders. I also believe, because of the way we are brought up, we in the US, possess some of the *Emotional Intelligence (EQ) talents* necessary for leaders in business. Additionally, with our education and experience we are able to develop good *work disciplines* for various *leadership positions* and we have the ability to *communicate* this to subordinates in a positive way. My own *leadership discipline* also extended to my personal life and I can honestly say it made my life a lot more worth living. This all happened after I was fired from my very secure position at the age of 50. Hopefully this book will help younger people realize what I had to realize at 50 and help to prepare them to be the leaders the US really needs and to develop a *discipline* that helps them to be successful and happy both in business and in life. The process is not easy as you may have to change a lot of what you do to understand and cultivate your *talents* and create a new *work and life discipline,* but it will be worth it. Good luck!

Following are short descriptions of each of the chapters of the book and a reading list that will be helpful to the reader in understanding where some of the ideas of the book came from. Although it is *probably* best to read the entire book, remembering our *'shortcut'* method and what we want to learn, try to focus on the parts of the books I suggest. There is also a list of *stories* I like to tell about my life events that helped me be who I am. Hopefully these stories will help you understand more about yourself and expose your *talents* and *strengths*, as I believe life is just a bunch of *short stories* and we all have them, we just don't write them down. The last thing I want to drive home to you at this point, is to document your progress, write some of your own *'short stories'*, use the forms provided to list your *talents and routines*, and simply have fun doing what is suggested in the book. If you think learning your *talents* and developing a *discipline* to promote your *value* to the world is impossible remember what Walt Disney said: *"It's kind of fun to do the impossible"*[6]

<u>Individual Chapters</u>

<u>The Changing Environment</u> discusses how the world is changing faster than one can imagine. Some of these changes are not really conducive to developing a fixed, firm leadership discipline. The 'Post American World' is discussed along with the effects of economic, political, and cultural change. Changes in technology and science are explored to

show the continuing effect these changes have had on inventions and leadership opportunities. There are also discussions on future changes and how humans will continue to add *value* in a world of robots, and how leadership will change as we move to *'leadership by teams'*. Life is organic, dynamic and ever changing and that is what the new leaders will have to contend with if they want to be effective and successful. There are four books suggested for developing a basic understanding for these changes; "The Post American World", "Decade of Change", "Executive EQ", and "Humans are Underrated" These books and the daily news about local and world events provide the groundwork for understanding how the world is changing and how leaders must be flexible and dynamic. The chapter also discusses how the United States advantages in education and Emotional EQ can be used in developing new leaders.

__Understanding Who You Are__ provides some ideas for you to get to know yourself better. It explains the use of DISC in self evaluation and the 360 evaluation process that shows how subordinates and superiors evaluate the reader's opinions of themselves. The chapter also provides some ways of self evaluation to develop a more realistic and honest approach in helping you to understand your abilities, *talents*, and *strengths.* It uses some examples of professional athletes to describe what a *talent* is and how it should be practiced. It explores the readers capabilities in *curiosity, communication, executive EQ and imagination* by suggesting ways of testing yourself and documenting the results. There are forms to document the test results and suggestions to improve certain skills. The chapter is devoted to having you get to know yourself honestly; what you can and cannot do and how to manage around your shortcomings. It is the first step in getting to know what is *'worth writing home about'* about you. The chapter is intended to lay the groundwork for discovering your *real talents* and *strengths* by getting you to know and like yourself in a positive way, just as you are. It uses a lot of information from "Now Discover your Strengths", "Executive EQ", "Conscious Business" and "First Break All The Rules".

The chapter **_Talents_** provides the many definitions of a **talent and a strength**, and continues on with the positive aspects of **'Understanding Who You Are'**. It goes into detail on how a talent is born in the brain at a very young age, and discusses the different types of talents. It tries to help you learn and believe just what your talents are by using examples from the reading materials and a lot of information from "First Break All the Rules", on the different types of talents; especially from the chapter entitled 'Decade of the Brain'. It introduces some of the thirty-four themes from the Strengths Finder in "Now Discover Your Strengths" to help you have a way of **learning your own talents**. "Executive EQ" is used to provide examples and ideas on the emotional aspects of talents in helping you understand your talents. The chapter discusses the difference between **intuitive** or automatic thoughts (passions) that come to you quickly without much effort and **reasoning** that is effortful and slower, and usually without emotion. Understanding one's talents and using them productively is the heart of this book so it is very important to understand the origins of talents and how to learn to use them productively. The chapter also discusses **'Radar' or what I call 'Gut Feelings'** from the book "The Lonely Crowd". There is a discussion on how to practice your talents and recognize your weaknesses. You will learn about the Author's weakness that he has learned to work around by using **KYMS** (keep your mouth shut) when necessary. You will also learn how Tiger Woods and Michael Jordan practice and prioritize their talents. You will also learn of the Author's two strongest talents and others' talents in an effort to help the reader learn of their talents. The range of talents discussed is wide in an effort to show the reader where he/she may be able to add *value* in life. The range goes from *basic talents of honesty, integrity, etc.* to the *talents of the heart including empathy, social sensitivity, radar, etc.* This is, as I said, the heart of the book and really tries to have you understand the *value you can bring by knowing, believing, and using your talents.*

The chapter **_Discipline_** discusses aspects of both a *life and work discipline* in the use of *talents*. It tries to drive home the point of disciplining thoughts when using ones' talents by *removing any excess emotion*, and developing and practicing simple routines that become hardened disciplines. It explains that the *life discipline* includes the staple talents: integrity, honesty, work ethic, social responsibility, etc. The *work discipline* of talents is tailored to the particular position and includes the basic aspects of the life discipline and establishes a routine to incorporate the necessary talents to work consistently and most importantly productively. It discusses how the work discipline is developed to include the mission and goals of the company and is tailored to the leadership position the reader is trying to fill.

There is a discussion on the different types of disciplined people and how to control one's actions through *'disciplined thought, disciplined words, and disciplined action'*. The chapter discusses where some of the original ideas for writing *"Creating a Leadership Discipline"* came from and includes the thoughts I got from two books, "First Break All the Rules" and "The Discipline of Market Leaders". In "Break All the Rules" I learned how to recognize and use my *talents*; "The Discipline of Market Leaders" showed me how important a consistent and *disciplined approach* is to being successful. The chapter includes examples of *simple routines and value disciplines* used by FedEx and Wal-Mart in an effort to explain how to *create a discipline to use your talents*. It also has a discussion on *reasonable expectations* and how to evaluate others fairly. All in all, it shows that knowing and using one's talents in a disciplined, productive, and passionate way will produce a successful leader in both life and the work situation. This chapter is devoted to trying to **explain ways to use your new found talents in a disciplined way** that will yield good consistent results.

The chapter on **<u>Communication</u>** works at showing how people present themselves every minute of every day by communicating. The chapter provides considerable information on thinking, speaking, writing, and body actions while talking. It makes the point that **thinking is the beginning of all communication and has to be disciplined to be effective and positive**. The key to successful communication is to be as **positive** as possible and that starts with how you think about a subject or a person. It drives home the point of always communicating in a respectful way, never taking anything personally, never assuming what someone is thinking, and listening in a **mindful way.** The chapter describes how the truth can change, sometimes quickly, and you need to be able to react to the changes and have the record corrected if necessary. There is a discussion on people having all kinds of things going on in their life and mind and that you have to respect all of it by **mindful listening** and being **conscious** of possible problems without knowing the whole story. There is a discussion on how **you <u>always</u> get a second chance to make a first impression** when you are communicating, if you are willing to honestly apologize for inappropriate assumptions and remarks you make to other people. It discusses a method of communication called **'plain talk'** where good plain simple English is used to get a sensitive situation out in the open without regard for personal feelings or prejudices. The chapter concludes with thoughts on **'mindful listening'** and the importance that listening has in communication.

The 'Beginning' At 'The End' is the last chapter of the book.. It is broken into two parts, a **quick review** of the main points of the book and what I hoped you would learn, and the full development of **Your Leadership Disciplines** with examples to help the reader fully understand and document important **talents, knowledge and strengths**, as well as the **disciplines or routines** you want to follow in life and in business to promote your **talents**. Additionally it is intended to help you create any other changes in communication style you would like to make. It also provides some suggestions on how to practice your talents and how to create the routines you need to discipline your actions to meet your thoughts and ideas. There are examples of talents, routines, disciplines and stories to help the reader understand how each is used to better understand the value you can bring to life by knowing, and using your talents and strengths in routine and disciplined ways. There is a lot devoted to help you write down all you have learned from the book and ways to write some short stories that emphasize your talents and disciplines. The goal of the chapter is to **integrate the quick review of the book into the written life and leadership disciplines of the reader.**

The reading list:

"First, Break All The Rules"	how to recognize your talents
"The Discipline of Market Leaders"	how to develop a discipline
"Good to Great"	what it really takes for self improvement
"Now Discover Your Strengths"	recognizing talents to strengths
"The Post American World"	changes to our world
"Decade of Change"	more changes to our world
"Executive EQ"	gut feelings and how others think
"Conscious Business"	total awareness of oneself and others
"The Lonely Crowd"	psychological book on understanding people
"GHW Bush"	understanding intuitive talents
"The Four Agreements"	four good statements on communications
"Humans are Underrated"	the value humans will always bring to some aspects of life

Stories

Chapter 2
THE CHANGING WORLD

Post American World

The world continues to change in many ways and what appears to be more rapidly with the use of *social media*. As we discuss these changes, it is very important to recognize the effect of social media on that change. The truth is that change itself can change through the use, or mis-use of social media. What appears to be the truth at 9am can change dramatically by 4pm, just look at any daily fluctuation of the world's stock markets. The world's problems very quickly become business problems. When using social media we want to *get the facts, not the fiction*. What we really want to understand is how change affects leadership and the daily decisions made by leaders in directing other people, and how social media can influence those decisions. Change in a *leadership discipline* caused by business dynamics, technology, competition, the economy, globalization and such can be expensive and cause unrest in any team, especially if the reason for the change is unclear or incorrect.

The period of change we are going to focus on for this discussion mostly involves the past 25 years and concentrates on the last decade.

Without getting too much into a history lesson, there have been **three power shifts over the last 500 years** in the distribution of world power. They have reshaped international life, its politics, economics, technology, and culture.

The first was **the rise of the Western world** from the fifteenth century to the eighteenth century. It produced modernity as we know it: science and technology, commerce and capitalism, the agricultural and industrial revolutions. It also produced the prolonged political dominance of the nations of the West.

The second shift took place at the end of the nineteenth century and was **the rise of the United States.** It became the most powerful nation since imperial Rome and was most likely stronger than any combination of other nations. For most of the last century the US has dominated global economics, politics, science and culture. For the last 20 years that dominance has been unrivaled. During this period leadership positions for many aspects of life and business were almost automatic for those in the US. Our educational facilities, wealth and experience provided many advantages to those seeking leadership positions both at home and abroad.

We are now living through the third great power shift of the modern era, *"the rise of the rest"*, or as some would say, *"The Post American World"* This change is most dramatic in the US. It will more directly affect the way our new leaders have to consider change. Over the past few decades many countries have had economic growth rates at 4% or higher and, although mostly visible in Asia, includes many non Asian countries. As a result, many American icons have now been appropriated by foreigners. From the tallest building (Dubai) to the largest shopping mall (Beijing) the US is no longer the leader, and this is true in many other leadership areas as well. For those of us in the US things appear to be changing at a rapid rate and we are ***no longer seen as the automatic leader in politics, global economics, science and culture.***

This power shift includes shifting away from nation states where national power, both economic and military, has become less effective. We now have to deal with terrorists, insurgents, and militias of all kinds finding space to operate within the international system. Although these changes appear to be happening rapidly, in reality they have happened over years and a lot of them have been predicted. Our friend, social media, with its barrage of information on all kinds of goings on in the world gives the impression that this change is immediate, because that is the way social media works. ***It only considers what's happening NOW and the hell with how it came about or any history of the subject.***

A lot of the changes in the world that have to do with terrorists and violence have great impact on how people go about their daily lives. What may not be important to you may be devastating to someone else and effect their life tremendously. Again, be careful of how you use information from social media, ***get, and use the facts, not the fiction.*** Always remember, the world is changing and good leaders realize that ***"the worlds' problems very quickly become business problems"*** There can be a lot of leadership opportunity in that type of change.

Economic Change

"Over the last two decades about two billion people have entered the world of markets and trade - a world that was, until recently, the province of a small club of Western countries. As a result the global economy between 1990 and 2007 grew from $22.8 trillion to $53.3 trillion and global trade increased 133%. ***The so-called emerging markets have accounted for over half of this global growth and they now account for 40% of the world economy.*** [1] China and India will continue to grow, and even if they continue to be considered poor by others, when you multiply their per capita GDP by 2.5 billion people their total wealth will be massive. As their wealth increases, they will demand more of the world's natural resources like clean air, water, oil, gas, metals, etc. This will certainly change the focus and decisions of US leaders. In the late 70's and 80's we in the US enjoyed a pretty average growth rate in GDP of about 4%. Now we are lucky if we see an increase of 2% while emerging nations are experiencing the 4% and above.

This global economic shift and ***"rising of the rest"*** presents a challenge in that there will also be a shift in corporate leadership and cultural aspects of how we lead. Remember the golden rule, '***those with the gold rule'.*** Our new leaders will have to consider many new aspects of how to present ***leadership goals*** and ***communicate*** to a whole new ***diverse*** group of individuals. The changing economic climate for the US is, to say the least, challenging, and in order to stay in the game, we need to continue to lead, as ***leadership in any business helps us in the US to level the playing field economically.***

If we consider the overall life cycle of a product or service, from inception to getting it to the consumer to use, we see that the most profitable periods of this cycle are at the invention stage and the ultimate sale of the product (mark up). Although the production and assembly stages are important, they can usually be done by less skilled individuals, hence the loss of US manufacturing jobs to China, India, and others. In these changing times it is incumbent for us to maintain our advantage in leadership in all areas of business from technological advances, pharmaceutical discoveries, and business solutions across the spectrum of international trade. That leadership advantage may come in the form of inventions or business acumen. *At the heart of wherever it comes from will be a leader who understands and uses his/her talents and passions in a disciplined way. This leader will be able to communicate their technical skills in an emotionally intelligent way to lead their subordinates, be understood by their superiors, and reach their customers in this ever changing diverse society.* These new leaders are necessary at all levels in business and not just the CEO, CFO, or COO level. Good leadership positions occur throughout the organization and provide a solid foundation for many companies.

These global economic changes are not the only changes the US leader will have to deal with. Even if the leadership position is at a level isolated from these world changes, there are ramifications that have to be considered in our own back yard. It is not so easy anymore to get a good education, find a job, and progress up the ladder to a leadership position. *It is amusing to hear how 'our standard of living is always getting better'.* That may be true in some aspects of life in the US, but ask the average family of four where both parents work and the kids are farmed out to grandparents or other care givers so the parents can work. And then look at the family GDP and see what is left to put aside for retirement and the children's education after meeting the essential needs of food, housing, clothing, day care, health care, etc. Additionally, there are considerable fluctuations in the costs associated with every day life like transportation, housing, taxes and education.

Having an *economic life leadership discipline* that, at least, recognizes these fluctuations can be helpful in the challenging times to come. Learning what your budget should be, how to keep to it and make necessary adjustments will help to insure a more realistic and stable future. In short, *we in the US are going to have to learn how to do business and prosper in a slow growing economy at home with larger global concerns.*

Political Change

Whether you are liberal, conservative or whatever, there is always going to be political change. We in the US are fortunate to live in the most successful democracy in the world and what ever the changes, our democracy will remain stable. We still have the ability to get a good education, *understand and develop our talents*, and *create a discipline* to take advantage of those talents in becoming leaders.

It is always good to keep abreast of just what is going on in politics at the local, state, federal and world levels, as changes and unfortunately, news of wars, uprisings, terrorist attacks, etc. can have devastating affects on people in life and business decisions. *One should always remember that the world has endured many larger and more destructive times than those we are faced with today.* The whole idea of shifting away from nation states to rogue type governments, insurgents, and terrorist groups is scary and unsettling. It can also influence how we plan and develop leadership techniques. And, with the help of our good friend *social media* we can keep really up to date on the *facts or the fiction* of what is really happening.

Always remember that, unfortunately*, over sixteen million people died in the First World War, and over sixty million died in the Second World War.* As sad as it is to state, *one small group of Germans killed six million Jews in just seven years.* What we have seen more recently is much less scary and unsettling than what our parents and grandparents withstood due, in part, to the number of people affected by recent horrific events. ***The 911 attack killed 3500 Americans*** and recent terrorist attacks account for devastation and destruction of much less than that of the World Wars and other horrific events. Believe it or not ***we are living in one of the more peaceful times in the existence of the world.*** Can you imagine being a Jew in Europe in 1940? Even during the immediate aftermath of 911 the fear factor of any American could not have come close to the fear in the mind of that poor Jew in Europe.

All of the above is terrible when we think of the events of the world in the last century or the last year, but we have to keep it all in context and learn to be aware of what these political changes can do to how we plan and lead for the present and immediate future. After 911, many people thought we would never get back to normal, and maybe we haven't, but we have come a long way in just thirteen years. We all thought the changing of the date in computers at the year 2000 was going to create devastating problems in life and business. Not so, we even survived that and the changes that followed.

Again, and again, social media makes more out of something than we can imagine. There will always be bad news and political change in the world, especially now that we have a more globalized world. ***A good leader should always be aware of those changes, but not afraid of those changes.*** As FDR said during the great depression of the 1930's ***"All we have to fear is fear itself".*** Be careful not to let fear of political change or horrific events affect the development of a good leadership discipline. More importantly, don't ever radically change your discipline in a haphazard manner based on some social media report of world happenings. It is always important to know what is going on and being said about what is going on as it will affect those who work with you and how they are thinking. ***Learning to understand how people are thinking during stressful times is part of an emotional intelligence skill some refer to as "radar" that can be really helpful in communicating a good leadership discipline.*** There will be more on **"radar"** in the chapter on **Talents.**

It is, of course, very important to understand how fearful events affect people that we work with and especially those we manage. Just after the 911 event I found myself on an airplane visiting all my offices on the East coast just to listen to the concerns of our people. We in executive management had no immediate solutions to alleviate our people's concerns, but we at least wanted them to know that we were there to help if we could. The comments I received from those people ranged from outright anger at those who attacked the World Trade Center to fear of what changes may be ahead on the world scene. Listening to people's concerns during these visits drove home the point to me about ***just how important people are to everything we do and how important their well being is to any company.*** "Executive EQ" and "Conscious Business" have some good ideas on leadership and understanding people through 'emotional intelligence'. ***Listening, mindfully, to the concerns of those you work with is a big step in helping to make you a 'conscious leader' and someone to be trusted.***

Technical/Science Change

One of my reasons for writing this book is to help the person with a technical education and background become a better candidate for a leadership position. ***A technical education usually includes some courses that are based on performing tasks in an orderly fashion.*** Some would see this as a ***routine, or disciplined approach*** to solving a problem: hence, ***"Leadership Discipline".*** Developing a ***discipline*** to use our ***talents*** is much like developing a technical approach or "orderly fashion" to solving a problem. In discussing technical changes, it is important to note how technical education has evolved with the massive changes in technology that have occurred in the last twenty or so years.

For history's sake, there used to be a thing called a ***slide rule*** for calculating numbers. Now there are computers that you simply talk to for the answer, and if you are incorrect in your presentation, the computer will tell you so before you get too far down the ***orderly fashioned*** way of solving the problem. The computer will also tell you which orderly fashion you should be using.

Fifteen years ago I sat on a plane between two young computer sales people, one from Dell and one from Microsoft. I asked each of them what life expectancy I should consider for new computers I wanted to buy for my office. One of the sales people asked. "Why would you buy computers, you should be renting them?" The other person agreed and said "Don't rent them for more than six months because they will be outdated in that time." That was fifteen years ago, I got my new I-phone six months ago, haven't learned how to use all of it yet and thanks to Apple, as they change the software automatically, it is not yet obsolete. It also gives me newer technology to keep abreast of the latest techniques in communicating with people.

The technical and science changes the world has had, especially in the last hundred years or so, have led to ***enormous changes in how we work and especially how we lead others.*** When one considers earlier technological changes like the telephone, the assembly line, the printing press, and the internal combustion engine, or changes in science like pharmaceuticals, medicine and the like it is easier to understand why such world-altering advances that alter the way humans live work and even think of humanity take so much time to fully develop. The first telephone was used by getting an operator and giving her a number and then being connected. Now, saying "call home" while driving in your car accomplishes the same, and the changes over the years included the dial phone, the touch tone phone, the voice activated phone and now probably the phone that will dial if you just think of the number, not to mention all the other things your phone can do. All of this started with the simple idea of talking to someone who wasn't in the same room.

We could detail many inventions in technology and science in the same way and realize how much we get out of the *leadership and passion of the inventor.* Warren Buffet likes to say *"there is no finish line"*, and I think what he means is that if you really have a passion for your *talents,* you will always be thinking and inventing, and bettering others you are leading. Just try and think how many companies, jobs, inventions, profits, and increases in the standard of living have come out of inventions like the telephone, or electricity, or the use of the production line, or penicillin. These are all *changes and bring great opportunity and require adjustments in how we manage and lead*.

Now let's talk about one of the more recent technological changes that started as a *"military interest......to communicate over radio and satellite"*, the *internet,* that some believe "is the greatest advance of our age". (2) When you think of the changes in communications and the nature of business that have been born out of the invention of the internet, it is easier to understand that *"there is no finish line"*. Especially when it comes to advancing ourselves by using our talents (passions) and leadership.

As you have probably realized by now, I am not a big fan of some of the applications of the internet. However that is not true of many of the applications. My big problem is with social media and how facts can get replaced with fiction and how this can interfere with good leadership decisions.

Some think, and maybe believe, that **the internet was invented in a big bang way.** There was no internet and then there was. Not so, the beginning of the internet actually dates back to 1969 when the US military was trying to find a better way for ships and troops to communicate. The development to its "first rollout took over ten years and then another ten years to get to the point where the general public had access to it." [3] In this period commercialization of the internet was developing and in 1995 the growth of commercial service providers actually replaced the governments' backbone service for public use. **So it took over twenty-five years for this technological change to develop.** And some believe the internet is just getting started. It certainly has radically changed the way we communicate with each other, provided easy access to information as well as computers that talk to each other without any human interface.

Understanding and using the internet is essential for the modern leader, and keeping up with the advancements and new applications is also important in the development of a **flexible, organic leadership discipline.** Although the basic or fundamental aspects of a good leadership discipline may be etched in concrete, technological advancements provide change that will make any discipline better. Many **new talents and skills** for individuals will emerge from the various uses of the internet while people learn to automatically multitask in their daily life and work routines. Multitasking is another concern I have with the never ending uses of the internet. Although some really good companies encourage it, bring your computer to meetings so you can keep up with answering E-mails, there are some dangers, especially when you are trying to develop leaders who need *to mindfully listen and apply emotional intelligence techniques to their leadership discipline.* Multitasking is not recommended when a leader is consciously engaged with a subordinate or superior in explaining something or listening.

Enough on the internet for now, use it as much as you can and be careful of any pitfalls or poor information it may contain.

Other changes in science that need mention are those in pharmaceuticals and medicine, as this is an area where the US continues to lead and many opportunities for leadership exist. It seems like every day someone has developed a new medicine or device to make life better and longer for all of us. There are now personal computers that monitor life functions 24/7 and make it easier for individuals to take better care of their health.

In one recent effort to develop better antibiotics a device for isolating the bacteria was developed that will revolutionize the development of many new medicines. Changes like this are occurring every day and are exciting to know of and learn about. They also have great effects on how we manage and lead people. Just like the evolution of the telephone, or the internet, these inventions will have a long life and create many spin-offs, again bringing about change in the way we do things in life and business. Change of this sort can be interesting and exciting and good leaders look forward to finding advantages within these changes that will enhance their leadership abilities. *Just knowing and understanding what is going on around you will help make you more of a Renaissance Person and more respected by those who work with you.*

Cultural Change

"The most untapped natural resource in the US today is women." I put this in quotes because I like to think that I coined this phrase, but it was *probably* said by someone else long before me. The statement is true because when you have a population split of 50/50 among men and women and there are ten male leaders for every one female it would appear the women are not getting a fair chance at leadership positions. In the US, men and women are given the same educational opportunities, and are fortunate enough to be brought up in the same free *"Life, Liberty, and the pursuit of Happiness"* environment.

So why the big difference in the number of male and female leaders? The answer is simple, because seeing men as leaders is *"ingrained in the culture"* [4] and any changes would cause a great deal of discomfort in how we do things for those in charge, the men, and maybe some women too. It has to be very clear that comparing the abilities of women to natural resources is in no way meant to be disrespectful towards women. This analogy is used only to drive home the point that *men and women are equal, period.* According to the results of a test I took to evaluate my strengths, or talents, one of my strengths is that I see all people as equal or to quote the Strength Theme "Fairness"(Consistency) (one of my strengths) "You are keenly aware of the need to treat people the same, no matter what their station in life…". [5]

Women in the workforce has and continues to be one of the changes in our culture that causes concern in how we live, do business, and more importantly treat each other. For a long time in our history there has been a prejudice *"ingrained in our culture"* against women working and being equal to men. Although changing, this prejudice still exists in wage discrepancy and advancement to leadership positions. When you consider that we used to simply list our cultural prejudices as ***race, creed, and national origin,*** not even mentioning gender, it becomes easier to see why making women in the workplace equal in all respects is so important and how it continues to drive many issues in our ever evolving cultural change.

Many cultural changes to our society are driven by our ending long carried prejudices and learning to see all people as equal. There are also secondary changes to our culture caused by ending our prejudices and changing the way we live to accommodate these changes. Before women were finally accepted into the workforce, the mom used to stay home to take care of the kids and house. Not any more, when 'Gavin or Evelyn' (my grandchildren) finish school now they probably go to an after school program until mom or dad finishes work, or if my wife and I are lucky, we get to see them until their parents get home. This is a big change in how our kids are being brought up, due to economic and cultural changes.

There are many of these changes in our culture that are taking place in society, especially considering the globalization of the world and how that is affecting the US and our institutions. These changes are difficult for many to understand and accept, probably because of how ***ingrained prejudices*** are in our culture. It seems like every day there are major stories of problems arising from race, religion, sex, national origin, handicapped issues, etc. Recently there has been a prolonged battle in Washington over immigration to the US that has magnified some of the prejudices we have ***ingrained in our culture*** and it also appears that race has once again become a major concern especially among young Afro Americans.

Additionally there have been religious concerns associated with terrorist activities that have been really confusing and hard to understand. Is the movement in the Middle East based on religious beliefs or just terrorists taking advantage of the religious divides that have existed for centuries? We are probably not going to answer that question in this book.

The cultural changes and the secondary changes, similar to mom going to work, that we are seeing in the US and throughout the world have a definite effect on our lives and the way we develop and administer any *leadership discipline*. We in the Western World have certain prejudices *ingrained in our culture* on all of these cultural changes. Additionally, we are confronted with the problems every day thanks to the internet and our social media organizations. And although I do not like seeing and hearing about these problems, social media is a good source of information here, but again, be careful to know *fact from fiction.*

One of the first things you want to do is to *examine yourself and find out your prejudices.* Learn what really gets to you when you hear of some problem or a cultural change to your own beliefs. Your reactions to these problems will be automatic and it is best to know when to question how you are thinking and how you will respond. You may learn more about yourself by reading the stories, "Erin's Lighthouses" and "The First Chatham A's Game" at the end of the book under "The Stories" section. "Erin's Lighthouses" highlights cultural changes to an old Irish neighborhood in Boston and some emotional talents. "The First Chatham A's Game" demonstrates how emotional talents sound and how people think and speak of themselves.

Years ago it was a lot easier, race, creed and national origin. More recently we have dealt with the same issues and many more. What we have realized over time is that there is a lot of *diversity in our*

workforce and society. **Diversity** is a much more inclusive way of recognizing inequities as it includes all types of prejudices that we **have ingrained in our culture** including all the standard above, as well as gender, age, handicapped issues, more detailed religious and national origin issues, and others. In trying to discover your prejudices there is a great game you can use to help you identify and learn about your prejudices called '**Diversity Bingo**'. First you assemble a diverse group of colleagues. Then using a simple 'Bingo' card where you have written questions about various diversities in our society, you ask the group to mingle and get all the answers to the questions. **The goal is to answer all the questions by talking to various people in the diverse group you have assembled.** You learn a lot of things about diversity and you get to see that **all people have a purpose and are pretty much equal.** If you have some drinks and snacks, it's even better. Believe it or not, it really helps you to see where you have problems concerning your prejudices and our culture. A quick visit to the internet under Diversity Bingo will give you the information you need to play the game.

A recent study by the Gallup Organization that will continue for 100 years is trying to find out what one thing it is people, all over the world want. Is there something that all people have in common that would make their life complete? **The answer so far is that people want a job, or a purpose.** Knowing that, isn't it time we worked through our prejudices and opened our culture to accept all for what they are, and saw them as equals? George W. Bush has a great quote on the matter of immigration: **"all immigrants make America more American"**

Throughout this chapter on The Changing World, it seems apparent that one of the things that will probably continue to change is the way we see others and ourselves, **hopefully with 'fewer prejudices ingrained in our culture'.**

Future Changes

You can be sure there will be future changes in each of the categories listed above. *Those changes will bring about all kinds of opportunities for leadership positions and the need to have a good discipline to demonstrate your talents, strengths and values.* A lot of these changes will be driven by further development of technological advancements that have already begun, like the internet and advances in medicine. Others will be completely new and not even thought of yet, just like all those ideas that came from the telephone or the automobile. Developing a good *flexible Leadership Discipline* will help you to be able to take advantage of these opportunities at the right time. Please remember that good leadership is necessary at all levels of business and in all you do in life. Keeping abreast of what is going on in the world and business, economically, politically, technologically, and culturally will keep your focus on these opportunities.

There are a few industries that I believe will lead the way in future changes. These industries include those associated with *natural resources.* As the global economy changes to accommodate the *'rising of the rest'* you can be sure that innovation to meet the needs of this global growth will provide exceptional opportunity for new leaders who possess all the talents and discipline we will discuss throughout this book. There are two examples, of many, to consider: *one is water and the other is food.*

Water is something dear to my heart. Serving as a Water Commissioner in my home town for over twenty years made me acutely aware of the importance of being able to provide potable water to the increasing world population. Right now, in the US *we cannot guarantee an adequate supply of potable water to all that want and need it.* Can you imagine how that is going to change when we try to provide for all the new agricultural needs to feed the 'rising of the rest'? I know the world is 75% water and there should be ways to solve the problems, and hopefully there will be, but the solution is a long way down the road and inventions, technology and industry are going to have to come up with the answers and that will require **good leaders at all levels of the solution.**

Food and the distribution of natural resources to create the protein and such for the increasing populations is an area that will also require much research, technological advancement and changes in how we produce, package, distribute and consume the new food products to meet this increased demand. *Right here in the US about 1 in 3 kids are not getting the nourishment they need to sustain a normal healthy life.*

There is a really sad story I need to tell you to drive home the point about food in our country and how our children are affected by the imbalance in our economy that is helping to create more people at the poverty level. One morning a grade school teacher asked her class what they had for breakfast and the responses went from nothing to eggs, bacon and juice. One little boy answered *"nothing, it wasn't my turn".* When the teacher asked what he meant by "it wasn't my turn" he answered, "I have two brothers and two sisters, and we only have so much food, today was not my turn to have breakfast." If ever you think there isn't a lot to do to make things better, *remember the little boy whose turn it wasn't.*

Sorry for the melodrama, but you need to know there is a lot of work to do here and throughout the world and *good leadership qualities in business and life are really necessary.*

How will humans add value?

Continuing on with my concern about the children who do not have enough food and future changes you will be encountering, there is one future cultural change that stands out and makes a really good case for you developing a *life leadership discipline* that goes far beyond your Leadership Discipline to become a good leader of others. That is the answer to the question; **how will humans add value?** Better still, *how will you add value?* There is a new book "Humans Are Underrated" by Geoff Colvin that discusses the need for humans remaining in charge no matter how sophisticated computers become. There are some tasks that humans will insist have to be done by other humans. "The issue isn't computer abilities; *it's the social necessity that individuals be accountable for important decisions."* [6] You will never want a computer telling you that you have a serious medical problem, even though the computer may be able to diagnose the problem and lay out a treatment process better than your doctor. *"Only humans can satisfy deep interpersonal needs"* "We are social beings hardwired from our evolutionary past to equate personal relationships with survival." [7] And it is not just in personal situations like your medical condition. The same is true in the legal process as there will always be a need for a human judge to hand out important decisions. It appears that there are certain situations where *individuals in accountability roles*- CEO's and other executives, military generals, government and business leaders at every level- will remain in those roles for the same reason and not be replaced by computers.

As computers become more sophisticated and continue to eliminate positions in factories and offices, on construction sites and behind counters the need for good leaders will shift away form some industries and be more important in other industries. This type of *future change* in the culture appears to suggest there will be more of a requirement for ***talents and strengths in interpersonal skills and emotional intelligence.*** This type of change, that will certainly take time in developing, may also require leaders to work together in groups with other leaders in solving problems and those groups will need to have "deep human abilities-empathy above all, social sensitivity, storytelling, collaborating, solving problems together, and building relationships." [8]

Humans developed these abilities of interaction with other humans and not machines. ***Many of these human abilities are innate or intuitive talents developed at a young age that many people possess and others don't.*** For now it is important to recognize the need for understanding these talents or strengths and to know how important they may be in developing a ***good leadership and life discipline.*** Henry Ford once complained, ***"Why is it every time I ask for a pair of hands, they come with a brain attached?"*** This was at a time when the machines of the assembly line could not function without human involvement, now the machines do better without human involvement "As a result the meaning of great performance has changed. It used to be that you had to be good at being machine like. ***Now, increasingly, you have to be good at being a person.*** Great performance requires us to be intensely human beings."[9] "Being a great performer is becoming less about what you know and more about what you're like." [10] "Tomorrow's most valuable engineers will not be geniuses in cubicles; rather they'll be those who can build relationships, brainstorm, collaborate, and lead." [11] ***All the more reason for you to develop a flexible life leadership discipline that includes a strong focus on human value.***

Chapter 3
UNDERSTANDING WHO YOU ARE

"I can do anything better than you" "No you can't" "Yes I can"

Understanding Who You Are is the beginning of learning what your talents are and how much you recognize what you do well and what you don't do so well. Hopefully, discussing and documenting your education, skills, experience and strengths, as well as some of your shortcomings, will help you on the road to finding the *'four lane highways'* in your mind that make up your *talents*. This chapter will discuss some of what can be learned in the following reference materials: "First Break All the Rules" "Conscious Business" "Now Discover Your Strengths" "Executive EQ" "The Quiet Man". The intention is to have you honestly begin to understand just what it is that you do well and how that is associated with your *talents.* The chapter is also designed to focus on the *positive* and help you see that *Understanding Who You Are* is really understanding your *talents and strengths* and how you have used them. You haven't just been lucky to get where you are in life, you have worked hard and probably do not give your own *talents* enough credit for your success.

"I don't know"

Tiger Woods, Tom Brady, Serena Williams, Michael Jordan, Ted Williams and Peggy Fleming are, or were, professional athletes and if asked what their **talents** are, most would know the answer: Golf, Football, Tennis, Basketball, Baseball and Figure Skating. On occasion, while sitting at a bar or playing golf with strangers, I have asked people what their **talents** are. You probably wouldn't believe some of the answers, although the most common is *"I don't know"*. It is hard for me to believe people really do not know what they do well or what their passions are. After some coaching, the answers get around to: "well, I think I speak well" or some say "maybe I'm a good listener". I never get an answer like "I have a great curiosity and really like to learn" or "I'm a really great communicator, both in the way I speak or the way I write". If I can solicit a positive answer, there is always some doubt in how they answer. *"You don't believe your true self is much to write home about"* [1] or you have just never thought about what you do really well and worked on it the same way the athletes mentioned above have. Some say Tiger hits six or seven hundred balls a day and Serena Williams probably hits ten times that number of tennis balls, both practicing what they do best, their **talents.**

For our work in this chapter, the definition of a talent is *"any recurring pattern of thought, feeling or behavior that can be productively applied."* [2] It's easy to understand what our athletes' **talents** are and how they practice them. When is the last time you practiced listening? This chapter is devoted to learning about yourself, beginning to recognize and understand your abilities and how to turn those abilities into **strengths** that you can use every day *"The acid test of a strength? The ability is a strength only if you can fathom yourself doing it repeatedly, happily, and successfully".* [3] Most of our **strengths** are based on our *talents,* and our *talents* are something we learn at a really young age.

Who You Are

"This man was born to do, to fight for truth and win, and in defeat, admit defeat, without defeat within". I have no idea who said this, it must be something I read or heard somewhere. Remember this as we explore just who you are. Honestly understanding who you are, what you can or cannot do is really important if you want to successfully lead others. Knowing what you don't know is probably more important than what you do know. There are a lot of ways to learn about yourself and just how smart or challenged you are. Whatever you decide on *Who You Are*, in no way should be seen as any kind of *'defeat'*. We all have something positive to contribute and a purpose in life. What we want to do is start the process of learning what your *talents* are. The best way to do that is to understand yourself and have some knowledge of your limits and expectations. You may be reluctant to do this as *"you don't believe your true self is much to write home about"*[4], but that's okay, we really want to concentrate on the good and just recognize the bad. You haven't just been lucky, you have knowledge, skills, talents and strengths that you have worked hard to acquire and refine.

You can get the start of a profile of yourself from a process called *D-I-S-C.* It gives you an idea of your behavioral strengths, personality, and demeanor by evaluating your answers to sets of questions that are designed to measure *Dominance, Influence, Steadiness, or Conscientiousness.* These questions are designed to measure your response and categorize the findings into one of these four areas. This type of testing will not answer all the questions, but it is a start. It helps you to see and understand yourself and maybe understand how others see you and how you fit into your life, or your work group. The testing also gives examples of each of the four areas to show what you emphasize in your behavior. ***Dominance*** for example shows an emphasis on overcoming obstacles and barriers to accomplish results. ***Influence*** shows you have ability in shaping the environment by influencing or persuading others. ***Steadiness*** indicates an emphasis on cooperating with others to carry out the task. ***Conscientiousness*** indicates you work conscientiously within existing circumstances to ensure quality and accuracy. You can find out more about the D-I-S-C process by using the internet. Type in ***DISC*** and choose the site that best fits your interest.

Another tool used to help us understand more about ourselves and our ***leadership style*** in the work environment is a development plan called a ***360 survey***. This measures how you see yourself, how your direct reports see you and how your boss sees you. It asks a lot of questions on planning, organizing, leading, and controlling. It shows you the national norm of how many participants scored on the questions. Some believe this shows more of your deficiencies than your strengths. The summary of the ***360*** lists ***Strengths, Areas for improvement, and Leadership style/Potential.*** You can find more on the ***360*** testing process on the internet. Type in ***360 leadership assessment*** and choose the site that best fits your interest.

The idea of these tests is to start a process to find out how you work and fit into your particular group. They help you measure your '***Emotional Intelligence***', not to find out how smart you are. "How you apply Emotional Intelligence requires that we learn to ***acknowledge*** and ***value*** feelings -in ourselves and others- and that we appropriately ***respond*** to them, effectively ***applying*** the information and energy of emotions in our daily life and work". [5]

There appears to be a lot of debate on where **leadership qualities** come from. Some believe **technical expertise or specific knowledge** of the tasks you are going to lead is the most important quality of the leader, while others believe it is the **Emotional Intelligence** qualities, and understanding people that make a good leader. As is usually the case, a good leader has to have both and depending on the actual position, how high up the ladder, the mix of technical qualities to emotional qualities will vary.

Throughout this book we will work to learn and understand what the readers' **talents** really are and how one might be able to discipline the use of those talents to become a good leader. In doing this **it is important to have a good understanding of where and what we are starting with, and what you think of yourself.**

Starting the process of learning and using your **talents** without **Understanding Who You Are** would be like getting into a car that was running and stepping on the gas not knowing if the car was in drive, reverse or park. Where would you go, forward, backward or no where? Let's find out what gear you're in and **get you going forward in a positive way.**

Recently there has been a debate starting on the benefits of a specific technical education vs. the benefits of a liberal arts education. Some believe the **specific technical education** will give you a better opportunity to be monetarily successful by developing **knowledge and skills**. Others believe this advantage may be true for the beginning of a career, but the **liberal arts education** will win out in the end as the individual changes jobs and gets into **leadership positions**. When you look at the educational backgrounds of some CEO's of technically oriented companies this appears to be true. It is generally agreed that a good leader be proficient in the technical aspects of his/her work, but that person will also benefit greatly from a good background in the liberal arts. I like to *equate the liberal arts education with the Emotional Intelligence skills learned throughout a career.* Today's leader needs to be competent in writing, speaking, listening, negotiating, and influencing, as well as leadership characteristics including honesty, energy, trust, curiosity, imagination and more. Many of these characteristics' are not part of any typical technical or liberal arts education; they come from *Emotional Intelligence and intuitive talents* that will be discussed in detail later.

A good starting point for understanding who you are is to sit down, think through your background and document your knowledge and skills. You can use the form at the end of this chapter under *Your Documentation and Test Results* to record this information. Another way of learning about who you are is to write down the *'short stories'* of your life, remembering events and situations in the form of a story you would tell to others to drive home a point you are trying to make. Throughout this book, I will use my own *'short stories'* to give you some ideas on how to discover and discipline your talents. I suggest you do the same.

There are two types of knowledge, *factual* which is what you learn about a subject, and *experiential* which is experience you have gained using the factual knowledge. Consider the *factual* knowledge the alphabet and the *experiential* knowledge speaking the language using the alphabet you learned. *Experiential knowledge "is something you must discipline yourself to pick up along the way and retain".* [6] Your list here should include your education and specific courses, especially the ones you liked, and experiences where you have used your education. You should also list the other things you have learned and experiences that may not include formal education. A good example here may be something you learned at a summer camp or in scouts, like sailing, being a life guard or earning a scout badge in recycling. All of your knowledge is important and '***worth writing home about***'. After developing a good list of your ***factual and experiential knowledge,*** see if you can discover a few areas where you have ***brought some structure to your experiential knowledge***. This would include "formalizing all the accumulated knowledge (on a task) into a sequence of steps that if followed would lead to performance"[7] of that task. A good example of developing a skill is seen in the task of public speaking. Take the ***factual*** knowledge on the subject you are speaking on, and the ***experiential*** knowledge you have gained in speaking, develop a sequence of steps:

1. Always start by telling people what you are going to tell them.
2. Tell them.
3. Tell them what you have told them.

Follow this sequence of steps and you will be a better public speaker".[8]

You can continue to improve on your skills with practice and learning more on any particular subject. ***"Skills will actually prove most valuable when they are combined with genuine talent."*** [9] We will explore this later in this chapter and the chapter on talents..

The next step in ***'Who you are'*** is to think through and document how you rank yourself in the following four areas, (possibly '***skills***' of your particular personality): ***curiosity, communication, emotional intelligence and imagination.*** We want to understand where you believe you excel and feel passion considering these areas or possible skills. These four areas or possible skills were chosen from various books on ***talents, strengths, and leadership,*** and are seen by some as good indicators of a persons' ***basic talents*** and how that person is perceived by others. There are probably many other indicators that could be used to establish a persons' basic talents, and we will discuss some of them later. ***It is also important to give yourself a quick review of your honesty, integrity, and overall decency as a person.*** You can be sure that without these basic ***'good qualities'*** your advancement in business and life will be quickly derailed.

Another way to help you understand what some of your ***innate or intuitive talents*** may be is to think of people in your life that you have looked up to and remember what it was about those people that you respected or copied in your own life. There may be one outstanding trait that your mother, father, or older sibling had that you picked up at a young age and carried throughout life. You may have also, at a young age, really enjoyed the way a coach or teacher handled various situations that led you down a path of ***empathy, curiosity, of just really trying to do well at something.*** In a few books, it is said that the first President Bush demonstrates ***an innate, or intuitive 'talent'*** of always recognizing some of the people he meets with a follow up letter or phone call just to let them know he was very conscious of his meeting with them. ***This trait is probably a display of emotional intelligence talents like empathy, sensitivity or consciousness and is driven by his strong desire to be aware of others at all times.*** This trait has been responsible for his many long lasting and good relationships with others. An important aspect of this ***'talent'*** of the Presidents' is that he learned this from his mother, at a young age, by watching how she responded to people in her life. As he grew up she encouraged him to follow up on relationships as she did. Having seen her example at a young age, when ***talents*** are being developed, it was easy for him to do.

This particular *'consciousness talent'* the President developed would remain with him through life and showed up as *'sensitivity'* when he was dealing with Soviet President Gorbachev during the fall of the Berlin Wall and the break up of the Soviet Union. Other world leaders wanted the President to 'gloat' over the misfortune of President Gorbachev by going to Berlin and *'dancing'* on the rubble of the wall just to rub it in and embarrass the man. President Bush wanted no part of any such act. He was too *'sensitive'* to the feelings and emotions of the Soviet President to even consider such a heartless gesture. President Bush continued this posture throughout the years of the Soviet Union breakup. He became a good friend of President Gorbachev and was probably the real leader in ending the 'cold war'. In much simpler terms, President Bush stuck to his *'consciousness talent'* to *"do the right thing"*. As time went on, he maintained this positive attitude towards President Gorbachev by going even further and being sure nothing embarrassing happened in the relationship. I like to modify the *"do the right thing"* by adding *'it doesn't have to happen'*. If you really stick to your talents, you consider actions that could occur in the future when you make a decision. My leadership discipline strongly includes, *'do the right thing, it doesn't have to happen'* to try and go further with being and staying *positive* in all that I do. A good example of this can be found in the short story at the end of the book entitled "The Flight Attendant". It tells a story of a time when I put some strong emotions of anger aside to remain positive.

As you can see, there are many ways to discover your *talents, skills, and strengths, and to discover just 'who you are'*. You may even find that you do possess *'something to write home about'* and it may be something you learned at a very young age. Now let's get on with looking at the four areas of your personality to see where you excel.

Curiosity

The first example of a measurement that some believe is a good way of understanding a persons capabilities in business, or life for that matter, is *curiosity*. I know it "killed the cat", and too much might be dangerous, but it does help to understand a persons interests in bettering themselves and their ambition. A *curious* person is honestly interested in learning new things all the time. When the curious person undertakes a task, he/she is interested in learning ways of doing that task better or differently *(improving their skills)* all the time to make the results better. They are *mindfully* involved in each aspect of the task to understand what they are doing and the best way for them to accomplish the goals of that task. These tasks do not have to be job related, they can be the routine work of cleaning the house or washing the car. Another way of measuring *curiosity* is to consider how you question information you receive on work or life related interests. This is an indication of your conscious effort to increase your knowledge on a particular subject and improve your skill in that area. How about you, what is your level of curiosity? Think about how you do things, and not just work related tasks. Are you *conscious and mindfully* involved in what you are doing, or are you just doing the task to get it done? Is the whole idea of multitasking interfering with your ability to concentrate on what you are doing? As a start to evaluating your curiosity, consider the following questions:

Are you curious about the tasks you perform daily?
Are you mindfully conscious about what you are doing, or are you day dreaming?
When involved in a specific task, does you mind wander off the subject?
Do you generally question news reports, or social media information?

Do you receive news of new ideas in a positive way?

Do you welcome change to ways of doing routine tasks?

Do you enjoy listening to others ideas?

Based on the answers to these questions and your own opinions you decide what level of curiosity you have. You will find it helpful to document the answers to these questions and comment on how you think about them. You might want to look ahead a few pages to see how I think you should grade yourself on these four areas of your personality.

Communication

To be a good leader you have to be able to ***communicate your vision and leadership*** to many different audiences including your direct reports, your boss, and sometimes your bosses boss or even higher if you become a candidate for an executive position, and have to speak at an annual business or Board of Directors meeting. There are three ways to communicate: ***speaking, writing, or body language***. It is best to be ***positive*** as much as possible in any way you communicate. It also helps if you communicate positively in your life situations as well. There are always going to be times when the subject is negative and you have to get the point across, but it will be received in a much better way if it points out the ***positive*** as well. If you have to tell someone something negative about themselves or their work, you should make the negative part of the conversation about 10% of the total conversation and put it somewhere in the middle. Even though you are telling someone something negative, you want them to receive it positively, and that is easier to do if most of the conversation is positive. This is a place where Emotional Intelligence comes into play, ***"we learn to acknowledge and value feelings –in ourselves and others-and respond to them effectively"***. [10]

47

Many times, it's not what you say; it's how you say it. There are also times when no conversation is better than any comment you might want to make. The 'off the cuff' comment you might make at a meeting to show your humorous side or 'wise guy' ability, might be a big mistake that will long be remembered by those in attendance. When you are involved in a meeting of 'higher ups' you might want to adopt my simple way of reminding yourself to keep quiet. I write **KYMS** on each page of my note pad or computer while at the meeting. I am sure you figured out that **KYMS** means *Keep Your Mouth Shut*. When you develop the skill of being *mindfully conscious* of what you are doing, **KYMS** will come easy to you.

You also might want to consider a waiting period after writing something before sending it off to the recipient, especially if the writing is on E-mail. The time period can be ten minutes or a day, depending on the importance of the subject. I would also caution you on the use of texting, be careful of what you write in this haphazard way of communicating, it could come back to bite you in the ass when you least expect it.

The same is true of conversation when you have to deliver bad news to someone. You may want to rehearse the discussion and be ready to answer some hard questions. You may also give a negative impression with your body motions. Waving your arms or having a sour look on your face can say a lot to those listening and watching as you speak. Even your tone of voice can give the wrong impression. Where you pause in your delivery can change the meaning of what you are trying to say. Remaining cool calm and collected can go a long way in getting your point across.

Consider the following questions as a beginning to understand your communication talents or abilities. Remember to document the answers to the questions and feel free to add in other ideas or short stories you may have that help you to understand just how well you communicate.

Do you have a passion for public speaking?

Do you possess good writing skills, in formal reports, letters, or E- mails?

Do you prepare for scheduled teleconferences or do you just get on the phone and talk?

Are you a positive person when communicating?

Do you take conversations personally?

When delivering negative news to a direct report, do you accentuate his/her capabilities first or just tell them what they have done wrong?

Do people tell you the negative openly or do they fear repercussions?

Do you think about people's feelings when you are discussing things with them?

Are you a mindful listener?

Are you mindfully conscious about others when communicating with them?

Do you like to help people learn?

You may not be able to answer all these questions in relation to your work, but consider how you would answer in any life situation, like dealings with your family or friends. You want to know how, or if, you can get your point across in a ***positive, friendly manner,*** so people want and like to talk to you. All in all, do you like to communicate or would you rather not be bothered with talking to people? Again, just as with curiosity, you evaluate yourself to determine how well you communicate. If you believe you are not such a good communicator, don't worry, you can work on becoming better. Many people have used Toastmasters or other public speaking forums to improve communication as a skill. You will find however that how you communicate your talents, skills and values will be an important part of your *leadership disciplines,* both in life and at work.

Emotional Intelligence (EQ)

"She/He is a good leader, but just gets too emotional about everything, sometimes its' just not the end of the world." *Emotions* are something you may believe should be separated out from your thought process when making important decisions. *Not so.* "Feelings and emotions have a powerful influence on reasoning." *"Feelings have a say about how the rest of the brain and cognition go about their business. Their influence is immense."* (11) It is also good to understand that *emotions* are "neither positive nor negative, rather they serve as the single most powerful source of human energy, authenticity, and drive, and can offer us a wellspring of intuitive wisdom."(12) Understanding your emotional reactions to events and being able to keep them in context when responding to a particular circumstance is of course very important. You don't want to wear your *'heart on your sleeve'*, but *always acknowledge and value feelings, both your own and those of others.* Although this may be premature at this time in the book, I am going to quote a good definition of EQ that should be useful in helping you understand where you are when it comes to properly understanding and valuing your emotions.

> *"Emotional Intelligence is the ability to sense, understand, and effectively apply the power and acumen of emotions as a source of human energy information, connection and influence."*(13)

Almost everything you do in life whether it is intuitive or reasoning requires the use of some *emotional energy*. One good thing to learn is that some scientists believe *this intelligence is learnable and can be developed and improved at any time and at any age.* As a *talent, or strength* its' *value* will be able to be applied in work and in life situations. In simpler terms, think of "high EQ as someone who picks up-more readily, more deftly, and more quickly than others-the budding conflicts that need resolution." [14]

There is much to learn about the benefits of EQ especially when it comes to leadership. For years we have told people to check their emotions at the door and rely on basic reasoning in decision making. Now we are able to see that using Emotional Intelligence with reasoning provides the decision maker with intuition in the process, or as some would say includes the *'feelings of the heart'* with the reasoning of the head. Understanding where you are emotionally is a key part of understanding yourself. There is a good book, "Executive EQ" that provides good information on Emotional Intelligence in Leadership & Organizations. This book includes a questionnaire to help you determine your level of Emotional Intelligence. Although this book is one you should read, I would suggest you do that only after you have read this book as one of the things I was hoping to have you learn is what you should learn from each of the books listed in the Suggested Reading List that will help you understand yourself, your talents and strengths, and create your own leadership discipline. This book also includes a lot of what is said in *Executive EQ* and you will learn the basic message of that book later in this book. Right now, we want you to examine just how you deal emotionally with yourself and others. EQ will be a big part of what you should learn, and if you haven't already been exposed to using it as a major part of decision making, you will quickly see the

values of applying **emotional intelligence** in work and life. Take it from someone with a proficient EQ, when I realized the talent I had in acknowledging and valuing feelings in myself and others it became easy for me to understand the benefits of applying the **energy of emotions** in my daily life and work. It literally changed my life. I always thought I was ok, I just didn't believe it.

Now, with this little bit of background on EQ lets see if we can find a way to do a quick measure of your abilities in this area. It might be helpful to read the stories "Azel Road" and "The Ninth Grade Dance" in the section "The Stories" at the end of the book to see how the Author's emotional talents began and grew at a young age.

Once again, let's start the evaluation by asking yourself the following questions:

How many times have you used your '**gut feelings'** in decision making?

Do you feel badly when giving someone bad news about themselves?

Have you ever tried to '**feel out'** someone on a subject?

Have you ever said "I know what you are thinking"?

Have you ever heard the term '**Radar'** when discussing feelings?

Do you trust your relationships and teamwork abilities?

How creative and innovative are you?

How do you handle stressful situations like death or job insecurity?

Do you focus on peoples' **positive** qualities?

Can you sense the **mood of a group** when you enter the room?

Do you keep your feelings to yourself?

Do you lie about your feelings?

Are you proud of your work?

Is your life and work fun?

Do you have a sense of humor?

Do you wear your heart on your sleeve?

Again, answer these questions and any others you may believe will help define your EQ level and decide if you have a high, moderate, or low EQ. Remember, we only want to acquaint you with the idea of emotional intelligence. This is one of those places in the book where you want to be really honest with yourself as understanding your and others emotions is key to how you handle situations and how you will lead others. If you don't have these qualities, don't worry, you can find ways to learn and appreciate them. This is also a good place to think of a ***short story*** that may help you understand how you feel about yourself and others.

Imagination

"Imagine all the people living life in peace". Can you? John Lennon could, and he could imagine a lot more as well. ***Imagination as a value and a skill*** is something I really believe in as it has been a good part of my success. In my high school yearbook it was written that I could do anything ***'almost'*** just by thinking about it. I was also voted most talkative, so the saying, written by some "snot nosed" jealous English major probably was intended to mean that I was a BS artist. Fact is, he may have been correct, but later in life and especially in business, I could ***imagine solutions to technical and business problems*** that gave me a great advantage. I was also able to develop a very high level of ***Emotional Intelligence*** that allowed me the ability to sense and understand other people's emotions that also proved to be advantageous in both business and life.

For years I thought that statement ***'almost'*** defined me as a BS artist and I kept my ***feelings, beliefs and imagination*** to myself and did not use them in life or business. It was my involvement in politics that really helped me to see myself as a ***caring and emotional person*** especially interested in the wellbeing of others. I lost twice before finally being elected to a seat on the Board of Selectmen in my home town. After serving six years, I finally decided my feelings, beliefs' and imagination were ok and a lot of people, my voters, agreed. I could still be successful in politics, but George Washington was correct, ***two terms, period.*** Can you ***imagine*** how great our country would be if we had a law that said every office had a two term limit? That will have to remain in your imagination, because you can bet those in Washington are not going to change. That's enough about me and politics. Hopefully you will learn more about yourself if you listen to my BS, remember I was 'most talkative' and could do anything *'almost'* just by using my ***imagination.***

How do we measure imagination? Think of really good inventions and how they have been developed and furthered by people using their ***imaginations***; the advancements of the automobile, the computer, medicines, any imagination in the development or advancements in those areas? How about social media, remember '***fact or fiction***', it appears ***imagination*** runs wild here, maybe it should be '***fact or BS***'. Sit back and think of how many further developments of an invention you believed would be impossible. Imagine a car driving itself, some still think it is impossible, but it isn't because people used their ***imagination*** and had fun doing it. Remember "The future never just happens, it is created".[15] It has been said that "What we need is more people who specialize in the impossible" [16] so ***when you use your imagination, you are thinking of the impossible.*** As Walt Disney said, ***"It is always fun to do the impossible."*** It has been said that a "mind is a sad thing to waste" wasting an ***imagination*** is even worse as a lot of ***creativity*** is born in the impossible. Read the story at the end of the book entitled

"Pride and Imagination" for some ideas on how strong an imagination can be.

Measuring imagination is really difficult if you hold back your thoughts because you believe they are impossible. "Some people say why, others say why not?" Spoken by a great American, Robert Kennedy. Do you believe what he was thinking is impossible? Probably not now, but when he said this back in the 1960's a lot of people thought it was. Don't be afraid of who you are or of speaking about your dreams. Using your imagination just might help someone to solve some of the worlds' problems. A really quick way to see if you have an imagination is to think about how much you worry; after all, isn't worry just a negative form of imagination? Sorry about that, but if you can dream up things to worry about, you can probably dream up positive things as well.

Let's try answering some questions on imagination to get started on determining your imagination abilities.

Do you daydream about positive or negative issues?
Have you ever thought of a new product and then seen it for sale?
How many times have you said, that will never happen, and then it did?
Have you ever dreamed of the perfect vacation?
What kind of car did you buy when you hit the lottery?
How did you spend your lottery winnings?
What do you worry about?
Is it easy for you to worry about your health or well being?
Isn't worry just a negative form of imagination?
When was the last time you stopped thinking?
Have you ever meditated?

After you answer these questions, and any others you may have on imagination, you decide if you have an imagination. I will bet that you do and your problem is going to be using it in productive ways. If all you do is think about something, it will probably never happen. Taking the next step of talking about it and then possibly acting on the idea is where you will put your imagination to work. In your evaluation of your *imagination*, this is probably a good place for a few *short stories* on things you have been thinking about and never talked about. Try writing some of your ideas down and see how foolish they sound after you've thought them through enough to reduce them to writing; maybe you can do the *impossible.*

The listing of your education and experiences, your knowledge and skills, the people you looked up to at a young age, the four areas: curiosity, communication, emotional intelligence, and imagination is intended to have you start a conversation with yourself about yourself. Remember, we want to have you discover your real *talents* so we can help you develop a *discipline* to use them in life and business. Thinking about what you have done and writing it down in an orderly fashion is a good way to learn about yourself and commit to understanding just *what you do have that is worth writing home about.*

Your Documentation and Test Results

Your Education

List the five subjects or areas that you studied and you still have an interest in today. Examples: math, history, science, etc.

Your Knowledge

List five areas of knowledge that you learned at a young age that you still have interest in today. Examples: sailing, conservation, etc.

Your Skills

List five areas of education or knowledge that you have worked to perfect in the last ten years. Examples: public speaking, woodworking, etc.

Your Mentors

List three people you have looked up to in your life and what they have taught you that you emulate on a daily basis. Examples: your mother, emotional sensitivity,

your coach, persistence, desire to win

your teacher, confidence in your abilities

Your Honesty, Integrity, and Decency as a person

Give an example of an action using each of the above that demonstrates your abilities in that particular area. Examples: Honesty, giving credit where credit is due

Integrity, always living by your word

Decency, helping out in a food drive for the poor

Let's look at your test results of our four subjects by using a scale of one to ten to evaluate the four categories we discussed.

Curiosity   ------
Communication   ------
Emotional EQ   ------
Imagination   ------

I always thought a 'C' was OK in school so if you got all sevens or above you are *'probably'* well enough versed on these four categories and have a decent idea of **Who You Are** in these areas. It doesn't mean you have **talents** in these areas, but you probably do not think of yourself as a loser. If you got all fives, you 'maybe' **don't think much of yourself.** If your total score for all four categories is below sixteen, you may have a problem with self respect or your expectations of yourself and others are *'probably'* too high, or you are very critical of yourself. If you got above thirty-five for all four categories, 'you can do anything, **almost**, just by thinking about it.' This is only a starting point to get you thinking about whom you really are. We already know you're knowledgeable, skilled, and experienced, as you purchased the book and have read this far. I also think you are smart enough to know about your honesty, integrity and overall goodness as a person. If you don't have a honest 'C' in these areas, stop reading and throw the book away.

Now do a review of all that you have written above and see if you don't know yourself a little better than you did before this chapter. Please remember this is a fun exercise to help you **understand who you are**. You may get something out of writing a *'short story'* of all that you have documented in this review. It would not be a bad idea to write down the subjects you liked in school, the knowledge you have acquired, how you developed skills by expanding on your knowledge, something about the three mentors you admired, what you think of your honesty, integrity, and overall goodness as a person, and how you scored in the four areas we tested. It would *'probably'* be a pretty good story to tell, and you could try it out on someone close to you to see if they see you the same way you do. I'll bet you're not so bad after all. Remember the positive saying:

"I can do anything better than you" No you can't" "Yes I Can" is *'probably'* not a bad place to start in *Understanding Who You Are.*

Chapter 4
TALENTS

Now that we have a basic *Understanding of Who You Are*, we can dig down and find out what your *talents* and *strengths* really are. It may seem to you that we are repeating a lot of what we learned about you in *Understanding Who You Are*, and in some instances that may be true. This chapter is for you to learn the actual *talents* you possess, make sure you believe that you have these *talents,* and learn how important it is for you to use them to your advantage in both work and life situations. Reference materials used for this chapter include: "First Break All The Rules", (especially the information in chapter 3 entitled 'The Decade of the Brain' and Skills, Knowledge and Talents), "Now Discover Your Strengths" (especially the Strengths Finder listing), "Emotional EQ", "41 A Portrait Of My Father" and "The Lonely Crowd".

Maybe or Probably

Now that you have decided *'who you are'* we can continue to work at finding out just what your *talents* are and how to use them. I am sure that you all decided that you *'maybe'* have curiosity, communication skills, emotional intelligence and imagination. Still some doubt though, huh? That's okay, doubt is not a bad thing. Hopefully it helps to ground you and keep you thinking. Remember, *"you don't believe your true self is much to write home about"*. Just once I would like to ask someone what their talents are and get an answer that did not include a *'maybe'*. I know this is repetitious, and you are *'probably'* sick of listening to me say it, but in discovering your talents, you have to loose the *'maybe'*. Learning your *talents* is not enough; you have to believe in yourself and work to promote yourself through the use of your *talents* in a *disciplined* way. Not an easy thing to do, so lets try to introduce the word *'probably'* in describing just how well you do something. I did not say "you are *absolutely* sick of listening to me" I used *'probably'* to be able to keep my mind open to how you really feel without involving my ego in being correct. Instead of using the doubt word *'maybe'* lets try the word that keeps our ego out of any descriptions of our capabilities or opinions and has a more *positive* connotation. Instead of going from doubt to absolute on what our *talents* are, lets try going from doubt to *'probably'* when we describe our talents. If you are *'absolutely'* correct on a subject you can't accept new ideas on that subject without defeating your ego. If you are only *'probably'* correct, new information or ideas flow into your mind in a much more acceptable way.

I had an advisor once who pointed out to me how I, or anyone else, (in my opinion) had to be *'absolutely'* correct. He told me the use of *'absolutely'* came from my Christian upbringing as a Catholic. When I told him I was not a Catholic, he said, "oh, sorry, you must be Episcopalian". He was right, and he went on to say some Christians are taught to be *'absolute'* about religion, and that belief and teaching gets into our every day thought process. For a couple of months after that conversation, I put the word *'probably'* on all the mirrors in the house and in other places that I looked at frequently throughout the day. This may not seem to be very important to you, but believe me it can really change the way you see other people and especially their points of view.

"Keep your ego in your shoe" is a quote I really like, and using the word *'probably'* really helps you to do it. Defending ones' *ego* can promote anger, especially in a factual discussion, and anger can really dominate the thought process and interfere with good reasoning. Feelings, like anger, can cloud your reasoning ability and make it difficult to properly use your *talents.* The basic idea of this book is to help you learn what your *talents* are, and how to use them in a *disciplined* way. The disciplined way includes clearing away the excessive or uncontrolled feelings or emotions like anger, joy, sadness, etc. and letting your dominant *talents* work for you in decision making, communication or just accepting new information. Let's remember, "many people don't appreciate what *talents* are let alone what *their* talents are. They think that with enough practice almost anything is learnable." [1] So, how about we really try to understand *talents*, learn what ours are, and see if we can't learn how to use them without the *'excessive feelings (ego) cloud'*. Who knows, if we're lucky, it will *'probably'* work.

Your Talents

When I first started reading about leadership and how to manage people the first books I read were "First, Break All The Rules" and "The Discipline of Market Leaders". Very quickly, after about a year, I thought, "Oh this will be easy, I'll learn my *talents,* set up a *discipline* and boom, I'll be a great leader". It's been almost fifteen years now and I am still working on *'Understanding Who I am'*, what my *talents* are, and an ever changing *discipline* that has to remain organic with all the changes in life and what is going on around us. There are also the changes in me as a result of the learning process and the aging process that have to be incorporated into a *life discipline*. Believe me you think of things differently at fifty than you do at forty, and you will think of things differently at thirty than you do at twenty.

After reading much more on the *emotional* aspects of *talents* and how emotions play into reasoning and learning, my definition of *talents* has changed considerably. Hopefully you will learn what I have learned in a way for you to get beyond where I am in a much more proficient way. I have *'probably'* read fifty or so books on leadership, talents, skills, strengths, emotional EQ, and psychology, all in an effort to become a better leader and person. Navigating these books and learning how to use them in discovering your *talents* is a big part of this chapter. I also spent close to thirty-five years managing and leading small and large numbers of people in some of the best engineering and construction companies in the US. My experience includes a range of positions from managing small engineering teams to leading and directing the efforts of eight hundred engineers, scientists and construction management people on some of the most prestigious projects throughout the world. The last five years I have directed the technical aspects of claims during litigation on projects with monetary values in the billions of dollars.

Learning my *talents* and how to use them has been a long process. Creating a *discipline* for life continues to be *organic* with changes and redirection. Just recently my wife and I agreed on a change in our discipline of discussing politics. With the 2016 election BS getting into full swing, we decided to limit conversations about candidates. If we do have discussions, there will be a big pair of shoes in the entryway of our house where we will both leave our *'egos'*.

One of the big changes in my lifetime has been our political process and my *discipline* has been altered a number of times to accommodate the changes. I wish I could eliminate any thinking on the subject, but I can't as I love this country. I attribute a lot of my success to the *'Life, liberty and the pursuit of Happiness'* that this country affords to all. Because of this passion for the US and the way I see it being governed my *'excess feelings cloud'* can overtake any reasoning ability and interfere with a good, productive, and informative discussion with my wife, that usually results in my learning something I did not know. She, as well, has well founded beliefs in this country that are worthwhile knowing and understanding. Eliminating the *'excess feelings cloud'* allows me to learn from her and expand my knowledge of a subject. I even dare to hope that she might have learned something from me. For the first time in 48 years, after considerable thought and discussion, we both voted for the same person for Governor of Massachusetts.

About five years into my learning process on *Creating a Leadership Discipline,* I started mentoring others in leadership and this was one of the ways of learning and practicing my *talents*. It was around this time that I started to really understand the definition of a *talent* as being *a special natural ability or aptitude* some would consider *innate*. As I continued my *talent* learning process the definition changed to the more comprehensive definition of *"Talent is any recurring pattern of thought, feeling or behavior that can be productively applied"*[2] that some may consider *intuitive*.

My early definition of a *talent* was much different and based on a more technical and scientific understanding without a lot of the *emotional* (feeling or behavioral) elements. In this early definition, *talents* are developed in the first fifteen or so years of a persons' life. The brain, at birth, has one hundred billion neurons. "These cells are the raw material of the mind and the mind is the connections between the cells called the synapses." [3] As the child ages the **connections between the cells strengthen**. Some become very strong and others not so strong. The connections between cells that strengthen are described by some as **"four lane highways"**[4] while the weaker connections are **dirt paths**. The stronger connections become the mental pathways and the persons filter (character). "They produce the *'recurring pattern of behaviors'* that make her unique".[5] These pathways become the basis of a persons **talents**.

The **four lane highways** get used much more than the **dirt paths** and define where the person will **excel** and where they will **struggle**. Some studies of the brain believe that all of this cell connection process takes place by the time a person reaches early teens. It doesn't mean the person cannot continue to learn it just means there is a limit to how much a persons' character can be changed. For a more detailed description of this, see "First Break All the Rules" "The Decade of The Brain".

As you can see, both definitions of **talent** include *"recurring patterns of behavior"*. After considerable study of the emotional side of talents, the definition I like to use is

'a talent is any recurring pattern of thought, feeling or behavior that can be productively applied, <u>with the correct emotional input,</u> and provides satisfaction'.

This introduction of **emotion,** or **intuitive thoughts,** into **talents** is really important. When you develop a skill through **experiential** knowledge *"it becomes part of that intuitive system of thought"* [6] and may actually improve or broaden your **talents**. Remember my early definition of a **talent** that likened it to a **four lane highway** or mental pathway that became a persons' filter. "All of these pathways were thought to be defined early in life."[7] Neuroscience is telling us that beyond mid-teens there is a limit to how much of a persons' character can be recarved.

There are three basic categories of talent: "striving, the why of a person, thinking, the how of a person and relating, the who of a person". [8] Each of these categories has its' own *four lane highway* that is pretty much set and will remain stable throughout a persons life. Considering the information on *developing skills* and how they become part of *intuitive* thought, it appears to me that *talents* can be changed or at least *enhanced* later in life.

I like to think there are two types of talents; *innate or intuitive*, that come quickly (almost automatic) and *reasoning or learned (skills)* that take more time and thought. As you will learn in reading "Emotional EQ" emotion, gut feelings, etc. are *necessary* in reasoning and decision making. They are probably part of many basic *talents* that people have created in the connections between the cells of their brains. These *intuitive* thoughts (feelings) that can be changed by learning *skills* have an affect on *talents.* The *four lane highways* have a *heart* that helps keep us in the right lane.

There is a lot written on how to discover your *talents*. Some believe understanding talents, knowledge, and skills will help to determine your strengths. This in turn will help you discover your natural *talents* from things you have learned and how you learned them. They believe that when you have built a *strength*, "you have perfected your *innate talent* with knowledge and skills." [9] *"To develop a strength in any activity requires certain natural talents."* [10] Working back through the process of what you have learned and perfected, you will be able to understand the *innate talent* you possess. There is a good discussion on this in "Three Revolutionary Tools" found in Chapter 1 of "Now Discover Your Strengths".

Others believe you should keep a record of your daily tasks and decide what you like or dislike doing, in an effort to discover your *'recurring patterns of thought, feelings or behavior'*. You might consider what you liked that your mother or father did or something that your older brother or sister did as you were growing up. You probably copied a lot of what you saw at a young age and created some of the *four lane highways* in your brain that we have talked about. This same process will work with a favorite teacher or sports coach, or anyone you respected as a kid. As always, a combination of all of the above will *probably* work best.

It is important to know what you are looking for and the listing of *talents* for each of the basic *talent* categories: *striving, thinking, and relating*, is a good place to start. This listing can be found in the appendix of "Break All The Rules". It is also helpful to understand the neuroscience definition found in "Decade of the Brain". The discussion on pathways filter, and character from this chapter is interesting and useful once you add in the "Emotional EQ" information. *"Strengths Finder"* in "Now Discover Your Strengths" is also a good place to learn just what *talents* are. It lists thirty four themes of strength and describes each in terms to help you understand the *talents* associated with the *strength*.

Following along in identifying your *talents*, "you can monitor your spontaneous-top of mind reactions to the situations you encounter". [11] Using this approach, some of what you may find is the following: keen *observations* of human nature, need for *precision*, finding *humor* in every situation, compulsion to **take charge**, etc. If you are drawn to strangers, you may be a natural **extrovert** or if you stay with your closest friends you may have a natural desire to deepen existing relationships. Let's not forget the four examples we discussed in **Understanding Who You Are:** curiosity, communication, emotional intelligence, and imagination. All of this will lead you down the right path to discovering what you do best and where the **four lane highways** or pathways are in your brain. Sometimes it might just be doing something that **brings you satisfaction.** It doesn't have to be intellectual, it can be cleaning yourself out of a room or making sure something is done 'just right' all the time.

There are so many things that go on in your mind all the time and the **intuitive** thoughts are definitely the best clues to what you really do well. Everyone has **talents** and uses them daily in their *'recurring pattern of thought, feeling, or behavior'*. Completely understanding them along with the skills and knowledge that you have gained will help you to know your strengths and your weaknesses and help you to live a more rewarding life. Once you know what you do well and your weaknesses, you will be able to find ways to manage around the weakness and hone the strengths to a sharper point. This is where I believe you will enhance your **talents,** just like Tiger Woods or Michael Jordan, knowing what your strongest shot is will help you in your game. Remember, they always **practice their best shot**. They do not dwell on their weaknesses.

Knowing your **talents** is just the beginning. Understanding how skills, knowledge, emotional EQ, etc. affect your **talents** is where the real work begins. This work will continue considering the *'Changing Environment'* and all that is going on around us.

It will probably be helpful to take a few examples from the different sources mentioned above to start a list of your **talents**. As you go through these sources it might be helpful to write down your first ideas of your talents. It will also be helpful to keep your list somewhat short, say four to six basic talents for a start. At the end of this chapter there is a form to use for helping to record these first ideas of your talents. The first source is found in "First Break All The Rules" and examples of the three types of **talents**, striving, thinking and relating can be found in the appendix of the book.

"Listed are the most commonly found talents with a short definition of each", to guide your thinking in selecting your own talents.

A good example of a **Striving Talent**, one that might help you understand yourself is **"Ethics: A clear understanding of right and wrong which guides your actions."**[12] You can easily decide if this is one of your talents by thinking through a number of instances where you have or have not been ethical in your actions. Do you lie to get ahead, or is the truth, no matter how bad, the best pill to swallow? Another example of a Striving Talent that might be helpful is **"Achiever: A drive that is internal, constant and self-imposed."**[13] Evaluating this is simple, are you your own best critic, and are you always trying to do better on your own? Is your finished product always only a B when you know it could have been an A? I once asked my boss why he never criticized me and he said: "I'm not getting into that battle, you're your own worst critic." He was right; my drive came from within because **achieving** was one of my **'four lane highways'**.

Let's try a couple of examples from **Thinking Talents**. **"Discipline: A need to impose structure onto life and work"**.[14] This is pretty easy to evaluate. Do you develop **routines** for doing various recurring tasks, or do you do the same task differently every time you do it*? "Creativity: An ability to break existing configurations in favor of more effective/ appealing ones".*[(15)] When you see how a task is usually done, do you look for ways to do it better, or develop shortcuts to get it done faster, or do you just follow along in the routine that has worked for years? *Creativity, Problem Solving, and Imagination* are good *talents* that can distinguish a person as a leader when used properly.

Finally, for looking at commonly found *talents* from "First Break All The Rules", let's look at examples of *Relating Talents*. This may be a good place to introduce some *Emotional Intelligence* into the exploration of *talents* as *Relating Talents deal with building feelings of support and gaining the approval of others*. Again, we are at a point in this chapter that in my estimation is where this book tries to integrate the idea that *talents in emotional intelligence* are an important part of the *innate* or *intuitive talents* that you possess, and essential to your *reasoning and learned* skills. If we remember the definition of Emotional Intelligence that states:

"Emotional intelligence is the ability to sense, understand, and effectively apply the power and acumen as a source of human energy, information, and influence:"[(16)]

we see that definitions of *Relating talents* include much of what is said in that definition. For example,

"Developer: A need to invest in others and to derive satisfaction in so doing" or *"Empathy: An ability to identify the feelings and perspectives of others"* or *"Courage: An ability to use emotion to overcome resistance".*[(17)]

Many of the **Relating Talents** definitions are centered on the definition of Emotional Intelligence and my belief is that most talents, Striving, Thinking, or Relating, have some element of emotion or feeling. There are, of course, talents that have no emotional aspect at all such as **"Numerical: An affinity for numbers" or "Gestalt: A need to see order and accuracy"**[18] but I think you would agree that most of what we do best has some connection to the **heart.**

Continuing on the task of developing a list of your **talents,** the next source to consider is the **Strengths Finder Profile** included in "Now Discover Your Strengths". This way of discovering and understanding **talents** is designed to help you understand your **strengths** and ultimately your **talents** through a series of questions that measure your response to thirty-four themes of strengths that will help you **"find where you have the greatest potential for a strength."** [19] These thirty-four themes of talent were developed during a long study of excellence. "Once you complete the Strength Finder Profile you will receive your five most dominant **themes of talent**, your **signature them**es. These themes of talent may not yet be strengths. Each theme is a recurring pattern of thought, feeling, or behavior—the promise of a strength."[20] The book lists all thirty-four themes and you can read through them and try to evaluate what strengths or talents you may possess. I suggest you buy the book and take the profile to help you get started on your signature themes. When I took the profile, it was helpful and reading and understanding the various themes was also very helpful in showing me some of my weaknesses. As an example of reading through the themes to see if you possess particular strengths, lets take the theme **Communication**. Without quoting the entire definition of the theme, the highlights include the following: **"You like to explain, to describe, to host, to speak in public.…. You believe people have a very short** *attention span. They are bombarded by information, but very little of it survives. You want your information – whether an idea, an event, a product's features and benefits, a discovery or a lesson-to survive."*[21]

The theme goes on and gives examples of what **Communication sounds like**. Again not to quote all of what is said in the theme, **"Communication sounds like this: Stories are the best way to make my point…I resorted to imagery…talk only about things you are passionate about and always use personal examples."** [22] Each theme is presented in a similar way, first a definition of the strength and then what people who possess that theme sound like when they are describing their talent. Discovering your actual talents through the Strength Finders Profile takes time and effort, but the Strengths Finder was actually created to **"help you sharpen your perception. It presents you with pairs of statements, captures your choices, sorts them, and reflects back your most dominant patterns of behavior, thereby highlighting where you have the greatest potential for real strength."**[23] As you may recall, our definition of a **talent** includes the idea of '**patterns of behavior**' in the form of '**recurring pattern of thought**'. The process used by Strengths Finder helps to '**sharpen your perception**' on those recurring patterns of thought, or your talents. The **Strengths Finder Profile** is well worth the time and effort to help you with your list of talents.

Another way of **"pinpointing your talents is to monitor your behavior and your feelings over a period of time paying particular attention…. to spontaneous reactions, yearnings, rapid learning, and satisfactions."** [24] This method is the most time intensive but will also yield good results. Getting a good idea of just what talents, strengths, skills and knowledge are is very helpful in recognizing and understanding your innate or intuitive talents and also getting to know your reasoning or learned skills. Give close attention to the **rapid learning** aspect as what you learn quickly is a good indication of your **talents.** What you like to do (**satisfactio**n) is also a good indication of **talent.** When you add in the Emotional Intelligence aspects we have discussed you are on your way to listing your **talents** and **understanding your character as a person.**

This time intensive way of discovering who you are is very necessary in understanding your Emotional EQ. You have to know what you have inside yourself in the form of empathy, feelings and just exactly what you think of people. How much did you get out of being brought up in a free society that emphasized *'life, liberty, and the pursuit of happiness'* that will help you manage and lead other people? You can have all the **talents** and intelligence in the world, but if you don't have what it takes to honestly deal with and care about people you will not be successful as a leader. You won't even be able to lead yourself, and that is becoming more important as business shifts away from structured management and depends more on team efforts where leadership is found in all members of the team with less emphasis on the 'star CEO'. Look around, what is the one thing that we should care about in everything we do. It's people, and not any one class, group, or tribe, *it's all people.... period.*

Now go read the short story at the end of the book called Azel Road and see how I began to develop my *'four lane highway'* of **empathy** at the age of six or seven. Hopefully this story will help you remember events in your early life that helped form your **four lane highways** or dirt paths.

Radar

Now that we have started the process of **understanding who you are**, what your **talents** are, and what your Emotional EQ may be, its time to hone in on how all this goes together to develop a list of **talents** you can learn to understand and use to your benefit in a **disciplined** way. It is most important to have a good knowledge of how **emotions**, or as some would say, **the heart** plays into your everyday thoughts, decisions and actions. The mind is a very complex part of the body and in most cases acts automatically in thought. I sometimes get frustrated at trying to control the thought process involved with my **talent of imagination**. As much as using my imagination to fantasize about a **utopian situation** can be soothing and pleasant, the reverse, **worry**, can be really difficult to deal with. I can make the biggest mountain out of the smallest mole hill by just letting my imagination run wild, and trying to control it can be really hard to do.

In an effort to show you how the mind can control thoughts and actions, I am going to share a little test I used to use to demonstrate what was referred to as **"Radar"** from the book "The Lonely Crowd". **"Radar"** in this book was basically unconscious thought that we all possess. It was our mind reading what was going on around us and reacting through thought and sometimes action, just like radar on a ship or satellite. It tells you what is out there and if a response is necessary in thought or action. You may find yourself using it when you **know what someone is thinking** or at least think you do. And you may react without even knowing or thinking about your reaction. OK, so here is the test I used to perform on groups of people. These tests were performed at a time when a Jay-walking law had just been enacted in Boston, and people who walked on a 'don't walk' signal would be ticketed and required to pay a fine. I would approach a group of people waiting for the don't walk signal to change to 'walk' and just start walking across the street if there were no cars approaching, which still was illegal according to the law. When I got to the middle of the street, I would stop, turn around, and see that at least ninety percent of the people waiting had followed me across the street against the 'don't walk' signal.

I did this when I was about twenty- two while I was taking a psychology course from a great teacher (Elizabeth Williams). What I learned from that woman changed my life. I started to wonder about how and what I thought about and how to control my thoughts and actions to more productive use. Now, writing this book, and understanding how powerful the mind is, and how important emotion, feelings and *radar* are on how we think, speak and act, it is important to explain, as best I can, the power of the mind and the *'four lane highways'* that you have created. The people who followed me across that street had a *'four lane highway'* that said it is OK to cross because my *'radar'* sees that someone else is doing it and *automatically* the thought process said go. My belief is that there was about a nano-second of thought in the mind that initiated the action of crossing the street. The same is true of your *talents*, especially the *emotional* aspects, and how quickly your decisions are made. Great in some respects, but like my imagination, there is a down side. Learning control of these thoughts and especially trying to slow down the response can be difficult.

I can't say enough about the *emotional aspects* of your *talents* and how you have to understand and learn to control them to fully appreciate and use your talents. *'Radar"* is something you might want to understand to help you understand how fast the mind works and impacts your thoughts and actions. "The Lonely Crowd" is an old book that is well worth reading. It will help you with understanding yourself, your talents and how to use them productively. You can at least be aware of what is going on automatically in your brain in an effort to control your thoughts and actions just like I learned to **KYMS** in important meetings and not offend someone with a brash comment. Not very scientific, but it works.

As an example of using *'radar'*, the next time you approach someone and expect to have a discussion, let your *'radar'* kick in before you even start to talk. Look at how the person is standing or their facial expression to see if you can guess their feelings at that particular time, and see if you can't tailor your first remark in accordance with what you guessed is their particular mood. If they look angry or distressed you might want to soften how you begin the conversation. If they look happy and upbeat, you might want to join in with a smile of your own and a pleasant remark to start the conversation. After the conversation, do a short review of the conversation to see if your *'radar'* worked in helping you remain **positive** and productive in your actions. This is just one way of developing routines to try and be more **mindfully conscious** of yourself and others. Don't expect any great revelations from this example, just try it to help you become more aware of how *'radar'* is always, **automatically**, engaged in you and others. It might just be that *'radar'* is one of **your intuitive talents.**

All Your Talents

Completely knowing and understanding your **talents** is going to be a lifetime of work and the best way to start is by having a good idea of the basic **talents** you possess. Hopefully you have used the form provided at the end of this chapter to document your ideas on your **talents** from the suggestions found in "Break All The Rules", "Now Discover Your Strengths" and the ideas presented above. Start with the four or five **talents** you feel confident with and see if you can't get to understand where the talent came from, how you can use it to your advantage, and how to *practice* it in a *disciplined* way to understand it better. After you work on the four or five talents for a while, give yourself a grade from one to five on each and see where your *'four lane highways'* are the widest. This is also a time to start developing a *discipline, or routine* in understanding how to use and practice *talents.* As you evaluate each talent, do the evaluations in the same way. Ask yourself, what does this *talent sound like* to me? Where did this come from? Why do I like to do this, or what is it I like about doing this? How does this *talent* fit into my daily routine and where do I use it most? Is there a way to *practice* this talent in my daily *routine*, or at least a way to recognize when I am using it?

It may be helpful for me to use examples of two of my *talents* to help you get started; one example of a talent that uses a lot of *emotional intelligence* and another example without much use of emotional intelligence.

Communication is probably one of my best talents and it was one of my Signature Themes when I took the "StrengthsFinder". I believe this is an example of *intuitive talent* with emotional elements that are necessary in making it one of my *strengths*. The other example I want to use is a *Signature Theme, Significance*. This was my strongest strength and really describes me in many ways. I believe this is more of an *innate talent* and does not rely as much on emotional intelligence in making it a *strength*.

Communication

In evaluating *Communication* as a talent or strength, here is my answer to the question *How does Communication sound to me?* "Stories *are a good way for me to make my point. It makes me feel good to tell a good story and get my point across in a way that I feel really comfortable with, especially when I understand my audience through the use of radar".* Remember, I think life is just a bunch of *'short stories'* and communicating through telling stories fits right into this philosophy. As a kid, my *imagination* always helped me tell a good story, true or not, so that is *'probably'* where this *four lane highway* started. I like to communicate because I like to explain things to people and to speak in public. This talent fits into my daily routine, both at work and in my social life as leading people and providing technical expertise to lawyers (my present work) requires me to write reports that need to be technical and specific in nature. I like to meet new people and find out what they know that I don't, so being a good conversationalist is something I like to do. It helps me practice my *talent* in a social setting by remembering to be *positive,* use the word *'probably'*, and be a *mindful listener.* In my mentoring work I also get the opportunity to practice how I Communicate with people. I get feedback, both positive and negative from those I mentor.

In all of this I get to use my *emotional intelligence acumen* to enhance my knowledge and skills. There are good ways to practice your talents. Just like Tiger Woods or Michael Jordan, you can really build a talent into a strength that will help you in work and life. My obsession with using the word *'probably'* is a good example of this practice technique. It really helps me to keep my conversations positive and keeps the *emotional clouds* out of my reasoning. Mindful listening, something any good leader has to possess, is much easier to do when your ego or 'absolute' attitude is left in your *'probably'* shoe. *Communication* as a talent is a good example of combining an intuitive talent with emotional intelligence to create a strength.

Significance

Significance was my strongest strength when I took the StrengthsFinder. When I first read the definition, I was somewhat confused as it really covered a lot of different parts of my character. I thought the definition basically said that I wanted to be a *'big shot'*. After a few years of thinking it through I now see it has a very basic definition of who I am. When I answer the question, ***what does significance sound like to me***; the answer is easy; ***my life is full of goals, achievements and qualifications that I crave.***

I want to be known for the unique strengths that I have and I am continually ***challenging*** myself to do better. This ***talent*** is much more directly related to my abilities and not on what is going on around me that needs a lot of emotional intelligence. It is not devoid of feelings, but it doesn't use them as much in developing this talent into a strength. I believe this to be a basic ***innate talent*** with routes that go to my development at a very young age.

My brother Bill was a great athlete and excelled at any sport always being a winner. I was always Billy's brother and was expected to do the same. Truth was, 'not so'. The only sport I really liked was track, and that was running individual events, not team events. So, I knew I had to be great, but wanted to do it on my own, and by the way, I could always beat Bill in any running event (But that was it, he really was a great athlete). Here's how my *'four lane highway'* got built. My brain developed a deep channel or hole by having to succeed. It paved a couple of lanes with having to do it on my own, and it finished the highway with the competitive spirit I learned from Bill. I needed some semblance of victory, or for this story, ***significance***.

I still compete with Bill, our grandchildren are now a target for our competition, and they are all great. ***Significance*** became a talent and strength of mine, because with a brother like Bill I wanted to find a way to be seen or recognized. My work in this area became a way of life for me. As that boss once said to me ***"I am not getting into that battle, you're your own worst critic".*** My drive comes from within and started with competing with Bill. You might wonder why I like this. It really gives me satisfaction to be part of helping people succeed. Even when criticized for my positions I, at least, know someone is listening. ***"I want to be heard and stand out"*** and this really answers that need. It is a ***talent or strength*** that easily fits into my life in many ways. I always want to do better and know the second time I do something will be better that the first, that's why I believe you ***'always get a second chance to make a first impression'***. This is an easy talent to practice. I do it every day in most every task I perform. Always looking for the right, or better way, of doing something, or even saying something, or even thinking something can be mind boggling, but I truly love it. Just choosing the correct word to use when speaking with my grandchildren to keep them ***positive*** and learning things the right way is a real 'high' to me. Having Gavin (my grandson) ask me how to do something, or Evelyn (my granddaughter) ask my wife "where's grandpa" gives me a great feeling because I feel ***significant*** to them.

Completely understanding and practicing your talents can really pay off, both in work and life. I hope these examples explaining my talents, or strengths will help you to discover and understand ***your talents***. You may find some help in discovering your talents by reading the short story at the end of the book entitled "Five Women and One Really Big Little Boy". This story shows how ***talents*** are born and how they last throughout life. I know I can be verbose, but they're usually nice stories and you can be sure they're full of **emotion from the heart.**

Now go and work on **your talents**. See if you can list five or six areas where you believe you really excel and list the **talents** associated. Give yourself that grade from one to five **to prioritize your talents** and take a few days to let them sink in or try them out on work projects or on your friends. The big test will come when you actually admit to yourself that **you have talents**. Don't take this lightly; if you want someone to recognize or see your **talents**, you have to completely believe you have them. I know I **'probably'** communicate really well and I am sure you **'probably'** do many things really well. You just have to find out what it is and believe in yourself to do it. You live in a **free society**, you can think anything you want and work to develop real strengths from what you do best. Remember to always think of the **positive,** know your weaknesses, but build on the **talents.** Once you understand and believe in your **talents**, you can find ways to work around your weaknesses. As one Disney character says, **"ACCENTUATE THE POSITIVE".** You might want to read the short story at the end of the book entitled "Two Kids on a Plane". It shows you an example of staying positive in a stressful situation.

The Form to Document Your Talents

List four to six of your ***talents*** using this form for each one in an effort to describe the ***talent*** in a disciplined and consistent way to help you decide which of your talents are the strongest, ***'the four lane highways'***.

Talent or Strength _____

Source (where it came from) _____

The talent sounds like this

_____

_____

_____

I really like the following about this talent

_____

_____

_____

This talent is used in my daily routine by my doing the following

_____

_____

_____

I practice this talent in the following way

_____

_____

_____

My ranking of this talent is _____

As an example of using this form, go back in this chapter and see how I explained my **talent of Communication or Significance.** Remember, taking the time to write something down is one of the first steps in learning about yourself and your **talents.**

Chapter 5
DISCIPLINE

Learning what your *talents* are is just part of the battle. Knowing how to believe that you have these *talents* is where the real work begins. Then learning how to use your *talents* to your advantage is even more work. Throughout this process, having a *disciplined* approach to each step will keep you on track to *'Create Your Leadership Discipline'* for your life and work situation. In this chapter we will work to have you understand what the correct *discipline* is for you to use with your *talents.* Some of what you want to learn will be as easy as creating a simple routine for how you do everyday tasks. These *'routines will become disciplines'* that you control when using your *talents.* The reference material for this chapter includes: "The Discipline of Market Leaders" "Conscious Business" amd "Executive EQ". The theme of "The Discipline of Market Leaders" is about companies and the *disciplines* they use to keep their focus on products and customers. We took the liberty of using the *discipline theme* for individuals and how they *discipline* themselves to practice and use their *talents.* The companies discussed in the book were all leaders in their fields because they had developed and stuck to certain disciplines. The same can be true of individuals who know and understand their ***talents*** and create a ***discipline*** to promote their ***leadership values*** through the consistent use of their ***talents***.

KYMS

By this time you already know that KYMS means 'Keep Your Mouth Shut'. I have told you why this was important for me to adopt as part of my discipline. Being the 'Most Talkative' in high school and also somewhat of a BS artist, I was always wanting to tell the best story. With my ***Significance*** talent or strength I also wanted to stand out and be important. Although having ***Significance*** as a strength has some very valuable ***talents***, when you put the three aspects of my character together, talkative, BS, and Big Shot, it could also spell disaster, especially when I got to the senior management or executive level in my career. As I progressed in my career, it became apparent that blurting out a wise crack, or giving an ***'absolute'*** answer before hearing the entire question could really be offensive to the other people in the conversation. Even if my outburst was comical or contained humor, it appeared that there were always some people who found it offensive.

When I became an owner of a well respected engineering firm I had to go through an indoctrination of sorts. I was assigned to a more senior owner during a two or three day program designed to give me an overview of the company and how it worked. The fellow I was assigned to was a former test pilot and ran one of the companies' most important projects. He was in charge of 1000-1500 people. In a company of 6000 this was quite a position of importance. I had been told by others in the company how lucky I was to have such a person as somewhat of a mentor, and not to screw it up. As I prepared for the program, I went over my credentials and background and specific experience with the other companies I had worked for making sure I could dazzle this guy with my answers to his questions. After all, I had been an executive with a large Boston firm of 27,000, turned down two other offers from other companies to take the position with his firm and had actually refused to team with his firm on a major project in Boston. All that had to make me at least equal to or even superior to him.

Through all my preparation, the one thing I did, that paid off the most, was to decide to let him start the conversation. When he picked me up at my hotel on the first evening of the program we went through the pleasantries of introduction and then started to drive to a really nice place called the St. Louis Club for further introductions and dinner. He had never even gotten out of the car when he picked me up and for most of the drive never said a word. When we got to the club I couldn't wait to meet other members of the group to engage in conversation and start learning about the company.

After the cordial cocktail hour, we took our assigned seats to begin the presentations before dinner. The seat for my 'mentor' was empty and I soon found out why. He was the first speaker. As he spoke about his twenty-five or so years with the company, why he had chosen the company after the military, and the project he was in charge of it became clear to me that the best thing I practiced before meeting him was to **KYMS.** All of my acumen, experience, and even the BS couldn't hold a candle to what this fellow had accomplished, and he was only about five years older than me. During his presentation he told me most of what I wanted to know about the company, its history and the people who made up the executive branch. In fifteen minutes he had provided all I would ever have to know about the company. When he returned to the table and his seat, I shook his hand and said "Thanks, that was great". He smiled and said "Thanks", and that was about it. For all of my career one of the most impressive people I ever met was this fellow.

About two months after the program, I met with his boss who was the President of the Company, second in charge, and was visiting my office in Boston to see how I was doing. Boston was one of the larger offices of the Civil Group and a great place for people from St. Louis to visit. Over dinner that night he asked me what I thought of the program in St. Louis where I got my indoctrination. I told him how impressed I was with this fellow and how much I had learned from his presentation. He laughed a little and said, "Oh yea, Bob is a man of few words, and really well respected in the company". Then he told me that Bob had enjoyed meeting me, respected my background, and believed I would be a good fit at the company.

This series of events was probably one of the best lessons in **leadership discipline** I ever had. It made me realize the importance of controlling my **talents** and letting my ability to listen speak for itself. After learning Bob 'was a man of few words' I am sure his **positive** comments about me had a lot to do with my letting him start the conversation. This was just the beginning of my discipline of **KYMS**. There were many other instances where I would make mistakes and put my mouth in motion before engaging my mind. Knowing I had to control these outbursts I started writing **KYMS** on my notepads or computer when taking notes at a meeting. I also used to carry a thumbtack in my pocket at really high level meetings and would prick myself on the thigh every once in a while to remind myself not to blurt out something inappropriate. One thing about *'mindful listening'* instead of leading the *'wise crack parade'* is that you get to see the other jackasses in the group and how obnoxious they can appear when they blurt out something just for effect.

I hope this story helps you to see that you can **learn and create a discipline** for yourself in using your **talents** to a great benefit, just by starting with a simple **routine** like writing a reminder of what you want or don't want to do at the top of a note pad. Another lesson here is that when you start to develop **routines, or disciplines** to control and promote your **talents,** remember to '**plan your work and work your plan'.** Very quickly, you can decide how you are going to accomplish what you want and **create a plan** that gets you where you want to be. The success of your plan will be **sticking to how you work it with a disciplined approach. 'Planning your work and working your plan'** is the first step in creating a **discipline.**

One last note on **KYMS:** As I progressed and became one of the top sixty or so leaders in a company of 66,000, while at the Annual Business Meeting, I had a conversation with an executive about the presidential race in 2000 between GB and AG. He, knowing my political interest and philosophy asked who would win and what would be the deciding factor in the race. Without going into any detail, for this story, I told him how it would turn out right down to the possibility of the Supreme Court deciding the victor. He, in a place where he should have practiced **KYMS**, blurted out "that's nonsensical". What I, and other members of the group, heard was that he thought what I was saying was 'nonsense'. The next morning at breakfast, when discussing the political state of the nation, he asked me "Why so quiet", and I replied "Why would you want the opinion of someone who speaks nonsense"? After some respectful discussion on the meaning of 'nonsensical vs. nonsense' the conversation ended. I don't think my relationship with this executive ever recovered from that **KYMS** moment, and I still contend it was his **KYMS** moment and not mine. He knew my work on **KYMS** as he had seen the notepads and asked me why I wrote that and I had explained it in detail. Hopefully he learned a good lesson in that exchange, although I am sure he would never admit his mistake. For the record, the executive was and is a great guy and one of the best leaders I ever worked for. Oh, and by the way, GB did win the election and the Supreme Court was involved in the final decision.

As you go through the *discipline* learning process, know that some of the ways to create a *leadership discipline* can be as easy as establishing a simple *routine,* one that starts with *planning your work*, then practicing it, or *working the plan. KYMS* is not fancy, but it works and can help in many ways. It has helped me become a *'mindful listener'* and appreciate all I can learn from others. It is also the root of another one of my disciplines; *'keeping my ego in my shoe'* by using the word *'probably'* in discussing how much I know about something. This helps me to keep an open mind when discussing something and being able to learn someone else's point with little or no *'emotional cloud' problems*. The lesson here is two fold: a *leadership discipline* can be something really simple and you may find other elements of a good *discipline* when you work at, or practice, your *'disciplined talents'*.

YOUR LEADERSHIP DISCIPLINE

In the last chapter on **Talents** we dedicated a lot of time to explaining what *talents* are and how to learn just what your's are. In this conversation we explained, in detail, how many *talents* have origins that come from *innate or intuitive* thoughts that occur almost instantaneously in the mind. We also discussed how important it is to control those thoughts that usually contain a lot of emotion; anger, happiness, sadness, negativity, etc., especially in the decision making process. What you will find is, that with the mind acting as fast as it does using your *innate or intuitive talents*, this control is really hard to exercise. We also learned that your decisions need your emotions to help you act. Your *discipline* will have to be able to filter out just the right amount of emotion for you to make a really good decision. Developing a good *'routine'* when you want to use your *talents* is a good place to start.

When I first started to create my *leadership discipline*, I based some of my ideas on information in the book *"The Discipline of Market Leaders"*. As I stated before, "This is a book about the discipline needed (for companies) to become number one and remain number one." [1] I took the liberty of using some of the ideas of the book and applying them to creating an individuals' discipline. One message of the book *"is that no company can succeed today by trying to be all things to all people."* [2] The same is *probably* true of individual leaders, although they are expected to be really good at many things. When I began the work of *'creating a leadership discipline'* for myself it was clear to me that individuals' *'talents'* are the same as the *'value disciplines'* of companies that became Market Leaders. They create a *discipline* and use it to direct their business. The book used examples of some leading companies to show how sticking to their basic *'value disciplines'* in all, or at least most, of their business decisions was the right thing to do for their business. In an individual *leadership discipline*, knowing, understanding, and using *'talents'* in a *disciplined* way is similar to companies sticking to their *'value disciplines'* and a good start to *'becoming and remaining number one'*.

A good example used in the book was that of Federal Express and their *'value discipline'* of Operational Excellence; "providing customers with reliable products or services at competitive prices delivered with minimum difficulties or inconveniences." [3] (or for our conversation, to deliver by 10am) When FedEx was asked by a large proposed customer to change their 10am discipline and deliver to them by 8am so their service mechanics could have the parts they needed by the start of the day, FedEx did not respond in a positive enough way for the customer. Even though this would have been a sizeable new account for FedEx the response was not good enough for the customer. FedEx's response was driven by their *'value discipline'* of Operational Excellence to "provide customers competitive services delivered with minimum difficulty" or by 10 Am., not 8Am. FedEx did not want to change their discipline and tailor services for the proposed customer. They believed "maintaining their margins through low variety and high efficiency" [4] was the best value for their broad range of clients. You have to remember *"that no company can succeed today by trying to be all things to all people."* [5] The solution for the customer was to go to another shipping company, Airborne. Their *'value discipline'* of Customer Intimacy is "selling the customer a total solution and not just a product or service."[6] When I first read this I thought it was not a good decision for FedEx and they should have altered their discipline, but the more I read about FedEx and the other companies the more I was convinced that a *discipline* is something that you have to believe in and stick to if you are going to be successful. The same is true of a *"Leadership Discipline'*, you have to know your *'talents'* (value disciplines) and how to use them and stick to them. And, 'you can't succeed by trying to be all things to all people.' As you work to create your *leadership discipline*, hopefully, you will learn to use your *talents* in a disciplined way and how to manage around your weaknesses.

Another example was that of Wal-Mart and their *'value discipline'* of Operational Excellence to guarantee to be the low cost provider on all items in their stores. This didn't mean the lowest price of all products, it meant the customers total cost, including price, time in the store, convenience, etc. would add up to the lowest cost of the product all the time. At one point "when Wal-mart could have raised its prices a measly 1% …in an effort to add $800 million to the bottom line,"[7] it didn't. The idea was rejected out of hand. This idea did not fit into their *'value discipline'*; "anybody can hold a fall clearance sale, an anniversary promotion, or President's Day extravaganza."[8] Operational excellence companies trumpet their low prices every day 365 days a year. The reason: The idea did not meet Wal-Mart's discipline of being the low cost provider. "If it raised prices to exploit its current advantage, it would merely be stealing from its future success. Higher prices mean less *value leadership*. Less *leadership* means lower growth, and ultimately, shrinking margins." [9] Again, stick to your *discipline* and you will *probably* remain successful in your endeavors.

These examples of companies Market Disciplines are pretty old and I believe may have changed, as I now get FedEx deliveries at all times of the day and I can beat Wal-Mart's price now and again. The reasons for these changes go right back to Chapter 2, *'The Changing World'*. Purchasing on the internet has really increased the number of packages to be delivered and has lowered the price of many items sold by Wal-Mart. What isn't old, and hasn't changed is the idea of Market Leaders having a *discipline* for their business. I believe they develop their *disciplines* around what they do best, their *talents,* and where their business is in time and place.(what does their customer want) As changes in the world occur they may have to change their *discipline*, but it will be a well thought out change and not just for a particular trend or fad. You can be sure they will *'plan their work and work their plan'*. The same should be true of the *Leadership Discipline* you create for yourself; it should be developed to demonstrate your basic *talents* like honesty, integrity, timeliness, empathy, etc. that should probably never change.

It will also have ingredients that should be flexible to go along with the knowledge, skills, and strengths you bring to the position your are working at and the *discipline* or business controls of the company you are working for. The same will be true for your personal life discipline, there will be the basic ingredients and those that are flexible and will change as you grow older and your priorities change.

Understanding your *'talents'*, working to create strengths from them and having a firm *Leadership Discipline* to use them correctly will pay off both in your work situation and your life, just like it did for the companies mentioned above. Developing a good *discipline* for anything requires a lot of hard work and persistence. I sometimes make light of my use of the word *'probably'* or my *KYMS,* or even my *'keep your ego in your shoe'*, but they are all part of my basic *discipline.* I still have to practice them and keep them at the top of my mind when in a real life work or personal situation. One thing you might want to remember when you start a new learning process is to follow the simple advice of the saying *"plan your work and work your plan."* Doing this consistently helps you to create *routines* that will become *disciplines.*

Let's talk about some basic ingredients for a *Leadership Discipline*. The first one that comes to mind is being *positive in thought, communication, and action.* You can be sure that if you have a positive outlook on life, if you communicate that and demonstrate it with your actions people will want to be around you, listen to what you say and probably appreciate your actions.

Another basic ingredient is the meaning of my word *'probably'*. My definition of this is, *don't be too sure of yourself, but in a positive way*. Learning to use and honestly believing in the word *'probably'* is really important. It helps you to keep your *ego* out of your daily routines and life situations so that you can wholeheartedly understand others points of view in a way that does not threaten your beliefs. You should also remember the replacement of the word *'maybe'* with that of *'probably'*. Maybe, to me, means you have doubt in yourself and we do not want that. *'Probably'* on the other hand means you have confidence in what you believe and are open to others views on the subject. Believing in yourself is really important especially in knowing your **talents** and how to use them. Knowing, understanding and using your **talents** in a **disciplined** way also helps you to accept your shortcomings and learn how to manage around them. Sometimes knowing what **you don't know** is just, or more, important as knowing what **you do know**.

It is *'probably'* a good time to remind you that now you have an idea of what your **talents** are and are using a good **routine** to practice them daily, you have to remember to believe that you actually have these **talents** and you are going to create a **Leadership Discipline** to use them properly. One of the first steps for developing this **discipline** is to document the actions you take to practice your **talents,** and to record the practice sessions. It may start out as a simple routine like **thinking before talking, or waiting a few minutes before sending an E-mail or a text on your phone,** but they are all important and the more consistency you have in how you do it the better your **discipline** will become. Documenting the practice actions that you take can be as easy as keeping a small notebook and writing down the **talent** you have, the routine you used to practice it and how you thought you did during the practice. If you were practicing your *'communication talent'*, did you think before speaking, or did you just start talking to make your point to whomever it was you were practicing on? Did you **KYMS** when you needed to so you could also practice *'mindful listening'*. Did you use the word *'probably'* even in thinking what you were going to say to keep your ego out of the conversation? Documentation of your actions and reviewing what you did keeps you '*conscious*' of what you want to achieve and helps you tailor your routine so it becomes a *discipline.* You want these disciplines of how you use your *talents* to become automatic and kick in early in the process of using each talent. Just knowing that you have to be mindful (are you sticking to your routine or discipline?) of what you are thinking will help you a lot in your conversations and actions.

I know that I am '*probably*' a good communicator and I try to practice that every time I open my mouth or sit in front of this computer. I have to use the correct words to get my point across the way I want it to be understood. The *discipline* involved in this is my *persistence* in making sure I have used the correct word or phrase so that you understand what it is I am trying to say. You may not believe that I typed this paragraph and the preceding paragraph four or five times before I figured out the right way to say what I just said, and in the end, my editor will probably ask me to do it over as it is not clear enough.

The last two paragraphs involved a lot of writing to get to another discipline ingredient, *persistence.* This '*probably*' sounds like more of a *talent* than a routine to help you demonstrate your talents, but it really is a basic ingredient of developing a good *Leadership Discipline.* Remember *talents* are '*recurring thoughts or actions*'; the actions you take to understand and practice those talents require *persistence or recurring actions* to learn and understand what you do well. You should continue to document all of these actions and keep a record of the work you do. This way you can see your progress and adjust your *disciplines* to meet your particular life and work situations.

About twelve years ago I had by-pass surgery that caused me to change some aspects of my daily *'routine'*. It also changed my *'Leadership Discipline'* and work situation, but that's another story I may tell you later. After my surgery I needed to change my eating habits and exercise regularly to maintain a better state of health. Being lucky enough to have good wife who took care of my eating habits, by limiting my choices at the table, I was able to concentrate on a regular exercise routine. I started a regular walking routine of two and a half miles in the morning and afternoon. This took about two hours away from my established routines and adjustments were made in my time and activities. Each day I would record the miles I walked on a monthly calendar and then *'document'* the records to remind me of my goal to maintain a better state of health. I have done this now for the last twelve years, some years walking over 1800 miles and maintaining an average of about 1400 miles a year. When I started, before my surgery, I weighed about 185 lbs. and could barely walk a mile. Now I weigh 162 and still have a goal of 155 (what I weighed in high school). The point is that I established a *routine, or discipline*, that I have kept and documented.

Documenting your actions will help you to keep your *routine* so it becomes a *discipline,* and let you see your progress in making your goals. A good *'Leadership Discipline'* requires continual work and improvement and *'documentation'* to keep a record of what you do. It's like giving yourself a quiz every day on how you did. I still have a large calendar in a room near my bathroom where I record how many miles I walk each day before I go to bed at night, and yes, I still keep the monthly tallies and how many miles I walk each year. (2014-1616 miles, not a record, but not bad considering the bad winter we had in the Northeast)

Your *'talents'* are *'values'* and value is what people want and what leaders must bring to the table just like the *'value disciplines'* of the Market Leader companies. Leaders also must get all the *'value'* they can from those they lead. This is another place where a good *discipline* can really help. Having a good consistent routine or *'discipline'* with your reports helps to ensure good performance and respect for your leadership. You have to work at improving your *'value'* as a leader to continue to earn respect by building your skills and knowledge and those of your reports into strengths. This is the same as a company building its' *'value discipline'* into more value for it's' customers.

This desire to continually improve both yourself and your reports is a demonstration of another key ingredient of a good leadership discipline, *consistency,* where you treat people the same no matter what. Being sure that all are treated the same with a good routine will help you to see the *talents* (values) of others and their short fallings and give you the information you need to help them succeed. Another aspect of how you treat others is to be sure you do not hold them to your standards. It is okay to have *reasonable expectations* for others and yourself, but understanding people and their capabilities is best when seen through reasonable eyes. Remember you and others 'cannot be all things to all people.' It may sound easy to see others *'through reasonable eyes'* but it can be a challenge, as you probably don't even know when you are evaluating them using your expectations. Expecting others to perform using your expectations can cause you to see others in a negative way if they don't respond or act in the same way that you would in the same situation. They may actually respond or act in a way that could yield the same or better results. This is not to say you shouldn't expect a high level, or quality results in what you ask someone to do, just evaluate the actions and results in a fair and *consistent* way.

As the Director of Government Marketing for a large engineering company I had eight direct reports in my group. Most of the people fit my profile of a good marketing worker; outgoing, willing to work lots of hours, being out at night to entertain and attending conferences that required weekends away from home, really good communication talents, etc. Two of the reports were just the opposite; quiet, liked the 9 to 5 schedule, and really didn't fit into the group. During an annual review I ranked the two at the bottom and their raises in salary were not as good as the others. Most of the review was centered on the attitude of the reports and how they fit into the 'good' marketing person based on my **expectations** as the Director. Upon further review it was found that one of the two had been responsible for winning more of his share of the groups work. He had concentrated his efforts on a very large project and his **talents** of **persistence and consistency** had paid off. It was also learned that he was a really hard worker and did a lot at home in the evening. He had a young family and his wife worked nights and weekends as a nurse, so staying late and giving up weekends was really difficult for him.

The message is simple; know someone's' life situation, evaluate all the results, and make sure your expectations of them considers what they have going on in life. They may be more successful in the end doing something their way than you would be doing it your way. And always remember, if you have someone, including yourself, who values family over work, you probably have a pretty good person.

Understanding others brings us back to our discussion on the talent of **Emotional EQ.** A good Leadership Discipline is going to include the **"ability to sense, understand, and effectively apply the power and acumen as a source of human energy, information and influence."**[10] Understanding how emotions effect decisions is a large part of a good discipline. Knowing when to put the correct amount of emotions aside when using your *talents* will lead to better decisions and help you to honestly understand others and their *disciplines*. It may be your emotions that want you to abandon your discipline in an effort to 'feel good' about something when you really have to stick to your guns. Or it could be a negative emotion about a situation that causes you to abandon your *positive attitude discipline* and see too much of the down side of a situation. All in all, *emotional harmony* in your leadership discipline is one of the main arteries that your mind needs to keep open. *'Don't wear your heart on your sleeve'*, just remember how important it is and use it correctly. Be aware of the life situations of others. Remember, *the heart is more than just a pump*, its' "electromagnetic signals are transmitted to every cell in your body" [11] providing you with intuition and helping to keep you centered.

It may also be helpful if we are able to use our *'gut'* feelings *(radar)* in understanding others that we are trying to manage or lead. When you have used your knowledge and skills to create a strength and have a really good handle on how to use that strength through practice, practice, practice, you can get a lot out of your *'gut'* feelings or the use of *radar* in evaluating situations or the people involved. I know it is part of the Emotional EQ discipline mentioned above, but I think it needs to be an ingredient that we consider separately. *Radar* is something that happens at the speed of your mind and working to control actions driven by it can be really hard. It can also be extremely helpful if it is used in connection with a well practiced strength that you have. Just for a moment, think of the things in a day that you do automatically: how you think, how you talk, how you act, how you walk, how you eat, etc. etc. etc. The mind works so fast and so automatically that you, in a lot of instances, have no control of your response in a situation.

Using *'gut'* feelings with well practiced strengths can provide you with a great advantage and help you make the right decision when all else fails. Think of the benefit you would have if you could harness that energy into your *'Leadership Discipline'* and control your automatic thoughts.

This thinking may help you understand why **KYMS** is such an important part of my discipline. I haven't learned to control my thoughts as much as I would like, but I do a pretty good job controlling what I say and that certainly helps control my actions. There is a lot to be said about your *automatic* thoughts, especially how they effect stress in the body and this is not the place to discuss all that can be said about stress. I will leave you with one thought on the subject; when you can honestly stop worrying about something that really matters to you by using your *'talents'* and *'leadership discipline'*; you have good control of your *automatic thoughts.*

A summary of our ingredients for a good *Leadership Discipline* is as follows:

> *Positive in thought, communication and action*
> *Probably, not to be too sure of yourself, but in a positive way*
> *Persistence or recurring action of what you do well*
> *Consistency in how you treat others and yourself in learning new skills*
> *Reasonable expectations*
> *Emotional EQ*
> *Radar*

This is a good start on creating your *'leadership discipline'*. Developing *'routines'* to practice your *'talents'* will lead to a *'discipline'* that promotes your *'talents'* using the ingredients listed above, and any others you may want to add. When you get comfortable using all of the ingredients together it will become almost *'automatic'* in your mind or *intuitive* and you will have created your *discipline* to understand, believe and use your *'talents'* to your advantage in becoming a leader in your field. Always building on your *'skills and knowledge'* to improve your *'strengths'* will help keep you ahead of the field and remain a *'number one', or 'Market Leader'.*

Think Talk Do

Throughout this book I have told you to practice your *talents*, and practice your *discipline.* I have tried to show you ways to do that with some of my stories and thoughts. One thing that really works for me is when I have a new idea or think I have improved a *'talent'* or strength or a new routine or discipline for doing something, I really think about it for a while. I like to play mind games and try to discover flaws in my thinking. I actually consider thinking as a conversation with myself. After beating it to death in my mind, I might elevate it to the stature of talking about it with my wife, as she is my first guinea pig (poor her) and usually gives me honest opinions on my thoughts without applying her expectations to what I want to try. If it passes her evaluation positively, I might mention it to others or just act on it by doing something to see how it comes out. This can be a long process as I am a risk aversive person and don't take many chances, especially when it involves my ego, and that's what new ideas involve. A good example of this process is the writing of this book. I thought about writing this book after developing and giving a course called *"Creating A Leadership Discipline"* and completing two year long structured mentoring programs for twelve very talented young managers. The thought process took three years and a lot of reading to convince myself I really had something of *'value'* to offer those of you who bought the book. The thought process passed my wife's evaluation as well as my daughters, who is an author of three books on anxiety in young women. Okay, so now it passed the *'Think'* and *'Talk'* part of the process, now I had to act on it and do something. The best way for me to commit to *'do'* something is to spend money, so I took an office where I could go every day to write this book and do some consulting work, but the main reason for spending money on an office was the book.

You might be asking; what has this got to do with my learning what my *talents* are and how do I create a *discipline* to use them properly? That's pretty simple, if you think you have a talent, *'think'* about it for a while and try to convince yourself you really do have that *talent*, or blow it up and move on to something else. If you make it through the Think part of the process, go and *'tell'* someone that you *'probably'* do this particular talent really well. Once you *'tell'* someone you know will give you a positive response, go *'tell'* someone that doesn't give a rats' ass about you that you *'do'* something really well and see what they think. If you get by all the *'Tell'* process, than go and *'do'* what you believe.

Let's do an example and consider *empathy* as one of your talents; *you really care about people*. Okay, step one, *'think'* about it, how do you care about people? Do you care about what they can do for you, or do you care about their life and problems? What would you do to make their life better, if anything? Would you give them money? Would you take them aside and give them a pep talk, or would you just know they had some problems and feel sorry for them? How about a kid in Iraq who is going to bed hungry every night; you don't know him/her, you will probably never see him/her, and you probably can't help him/her, so why even think about him/her? Why not, he's a person just like you?

Okay, so beat yourself up for a while and decide if you want to *'talk'* to someone about the person you know and maybe the kid from Iraq. What are you going to say? How about, "You know, I think so and so is really having some problems with things and wondered how I might be able to help." Try something like this with three or four of your friends who know so and so and see how you feel. Do you like discussing the person's problems, or is it hard to start the conversation? Is *empathy* still one of your *'talents'*? Now try the same with the kid from Iraq. Same question, is it something you like to discuss, or do you shy away from it. Remember my definition of a talent;

'a talent is any recurring pattern of thought, feeling, or behavior that can be productively applied <u>with the correct emotional input</u> and provides satisfaction'

The emphasis here being *'provides satisfaction'*.

Ok, so you get some satisfaction out of recognizing *'thinking'* about the persons problems and *'talking'* about them with someone else. This probably means you still think *empathy* is a talent, so *'do'* something about your friends' problems. Go to the third step in the process, *'Do something'*.

Can you find a way to help this person? Do they need money, someone to talk to, or maybe just to be left alone? The answer isn't always that you physically *'do'* something, the answer can be that you care enough about the situation that you gave it a lot of thought and even discussed it with someone. Don't take this the wrong way, inaction can be the wrong solution, but there may be nothing you can do to solve the problem. This is probably much more true with the kid from Iraq. Knowing something and thinking and talking about it will most likely make you a better person and all the *'thinking and talking'* is not a waste of time. If you got through all of this, *'empathy'* is probably one of your **talents.**

You can use this process on anything you believe is a talent or part of your discipline, and remember, satisfaction is a big indicator of what your *'disciplined talents'* are. Going through the process of learning and understanding your *'talents'* and then creating a *'discipline'* to demonstrate and use them begins with *'plan your work and work your plan'.* When you start to document your actions in this learning process, you should also start to develop small plans with routines to accomplish each phase of the work. The important part of these plans is not how you write down what you are going to do, its to do what you plan consistently. A good example is how I planned each visit to my various offices when I was a Regional Manager. I planned to talk about **Safety, Quality, Financials, and People** at each office and in that order. Although what I said at each office was different, I followed the same routine, making different points specific to the particular office. This showed all 800 people in my region a *'disciplined approach'* to what was important for our business to succeed. Although they all heard the specifics of their office, they knew that **Safety** was number one, **Quality** was more important than the **Financials,** and **People** were what made it all happen. Ending with **People** was just as important as starting with **Safety.** At just about any level in my company, this was the routine that was followed. It became automatic throughout the different levels of management and I considered *'Safety, Quality, Financials, and People'* to be *'value disciplines'* of the company. Without going into the details of each subject, there were also similar *'routines'* followed for each of the subjects. Knowing the routine and following it made my position a lot easier and let me work on the real problems of an office in a structured and routine manner. Some of these routines will be discussed in the next chapter on ***Communication***.

Another important note on this example is that there are all levels of management and leadership and *'talented, disciplined leaders'* are necessary at all of those levels. Remember, I didn't write this book to create the next *'super duper' CEO*, I wrote this book to help the regular person who gets up every day with the idea of leading themselves and others by using their *'talents'* in a *'disciplined'* way that brings them and those they lead *'satisfaction'*, knowing that we all possess something *'worth writing home about.'*

Chapter 6
COMMUNICATION

Now that we have learned what your *'talents'* are and developed a *'discipline'* to use them to your advantage, its time to start talking about them and communicating just how smart you really are. Having determined that you really are *'something to write home about'* lets see if we can't learn how to say that in a way: that is *'positive'*, remembers that you're only *'probably'* as good as you think, and always considers the *'feelings'* of others using your *'emotional EQ talents'*. We spent a lot of time talking about *'keeping your ego in your shoe'* and no matter what form of communication we use, we should always remember to keep our ego in check. You *'probably'* are good, but so are a lot of those you work and live with and you now have the advantage of knowing all of that.

The reference materials for this chapter include "Executive EQ", "Conscious Business" "The Lonely Crowd" and "Humans are Underrated".

> *"You need to Accentuate The Positive,*
> *Eliminate The Negative*
> *Latch on to The Affirmative*
> *Don't mess with Mister In-Between"*

I know it is in a song, written in 1944 by Harold Arlen with lyrics by Johnny Mercer, that has been used in various movies when some director wants to drive home the point of being *positive.* I think it was probably written at a time (the end of WWII) when people wanted to get on with their lives after very long four or five years of hardships resulting from the war effort. I like it because it really drives home the key point needed for an effective *Communication strength and discipline.* I also like it because it was the year I was born and being brought up with that tune being sung in movies and on the radio, it has become somewhat of a routine for me when I need to remember to be *positive.* So, learn the words and the tune and start to use your discipline of being *Positive in Thought, Communication, and Action.* Sing it if you can, and if you can't, that's OK, singing isn't a talent we are looking for here. What we want to discuss here is how you communicate and that includes *thinking, speaking, writing, actions, and listening* with a *positive* attitude. We also want to start to put what we have discussed throughout the book into motion, or action. We have done a lot to develop the basic ideas and outline for your *Leadership Discipline.* Now it's time to start to use what you have decided is going to help you make the jump from a good manager to a leader, not just at work, but also in life. It is a time to fine tune your talents, strengths, routines and discipline and begin to get comfortable with your *Leadership Discipline.*

You can have the best *Leadership Discipline* in the world, but if you can't communicate that to others it means nothing. Although there are managers who will recognize your *talents* and hopefully put them to work for the team, it is very important that you wholeheartedly know and believe who you are and what your *'talents'* are. Communicating these talents and strengths through a consistent disciplined approach is key to having others recognize you for all of your values. This approach begins with how you communicate with yourself when you are thinking. Remember, most people believe *'they don't have much to write home about'* when it comes to their *'talents'*, so now is a good time to start your *discipline* of thinking *positively* about yourself especially when you are thinking through a situation.

The story "Two Kids on a Plane" under "The Stories" section at the end of the book demonstrates how important it is to stay positive with everyone you meet.

Thinking

Thinking is a very basic form of communication. It is no more than talking to yourself and developing thoughts and ideas to use for the other forms of communication. Thinking sets the stage for all communication and considering how fast the mind works you need to put some effort here to keep your thoughts *positive* as they will reflect your attitude in all communication. There's a good quote by Henry Ford that says; *"If you think you can or if you think you can't, you're right."* This quote shows how strong thinking is in what you end up doing in a particular task or in life in general. In our case, *'Can'* is the positive and 'Can't' is the negative, so even though we know Can't is in our vocabulary, lets put it aside for the time and concentrate on the *'Can'*, especially for thinking. Thinking is the first step in developing your attitude towards something and will also show up in your behavior on that subject, so it is really important to have positive thoughts as much as possible if you want a *positive attitude* and be seen as a person with *a positive behavior*.

Another element of keeping a positive attitude when thinking is always knowing that, in your mind, you are doing the right thing. You have probably heard the expression *'do the right thing'* in reference to your actions in life and the business world. I believe that action during your thinking process helps you to create and keep a *positive* attitude. Why think something through if you know how you are thinking about it is wrong? For our discussion on positive communication, that would be nonsense. One last comment on *'doing the right thing'*; if you consciously think of always *'doing the right thing'*, take it one more step and realize that you can add *'it doesn't have to happen'*. So the new saying for you to have in your mind would be *'do the right thing, it doesn't have to happen'*.

Using your mind in a conscious way is a very powerful tool in creating and keeping a positive attitude and to solve problems in a disciplined way. If your thought process is deep enough for you to, not only, *'do the right thing'* but includes continuing the thought process to consider any consequences so *'it doesn't have to happen'*, then you have taken a huge step in controlling your thinking and keeping it *positive.*

There is some good information on doing the right thing so it doesn't have to happen in the story "The Flight Attendant". There is also some good information on thinking in the story called "The First Chatham A's Game" under "The Stories" section at the end of the book. This story demonstrates how emotional talents sound and how people think and speak to themselves.

If you still need more validation on how hard it is to keep communication with yourself positive, I refer you back to the negative conversations called *'worry'* that you have with yourself all the time. As stated before, trying to stop *'worrying'* is really hard to do, but you can, or at least, you can put the worry aside for a while and get on with some positive thoughts. Try putting a time line on the subject you are *'worrying'* about and see if you can't decide to do the worrying later because it will be a considerable time before the *'worry event'* occurs and you may be able *"to imagine peaceful situations that trigger relaxation"*. [1] Now you have at least opened a door or window to let some sunlight in to your mind, and take advantage of the *'worry free'* time to get some *positive* conversation with yourself. "Dr. Herbert Benson, the founder of Harvard University's *'Mind Body Medical Institute'* calls this the *"relaxation response"*. Some believe that physical and spiritual healing take place when the mind is free of worry and the body is free of tension. Powerful tools for ending distress in the body are conscious breathing and meditation that help control your thought process and keep it *positive.* "You can relieve stress and stop anxiety with a deep breath. Concentrating on the breathing process immediately brings your attention to the here and now and soothes your mind. This is a simple yet very effective way to control stress." [2]

Worry Free

I was recently *worried* about a surgical procedure I needed to have that could yield some seriously negative results. The procedure was scheduled for a date sixty days from the diagnosis and my first thought was 'I have two months to *worry* about this, what a bummer'. After doing all the mental gymnastics and getting the facts straight on why it was Okay to take the sixty days to schedule the procedure(these doctors are really busy) I decided that the real *worry* or concern should be after the procedure and not during the waiting period. After all the procedure would determine if there was a problem. Being able to use deep breathing and meditation to step outside of my emotion of *worry* and look at the entire situation that was causing that emotion allowed me to see the situation in a completely different way and control the emotion of *'worry'* by relieving my stress and stopping my anxiety.

Although I was not completely *'worry free'*, I was able to get on with my life in a much more productive way and I got to do some *positive* thinking on my overall health. Next time you have a stressful situation causing you *'worry'* or anxiety, try getting outside the emotion by taking a few deep breaths so you can deal with the *'here and now'* and see all that is going on by putting your emotions in perspective. I know my stories are long and probably too personal, but I hope they give you some good examples to use when you are confronted with similar problems. Being a good leader starts with doing a good job with leading yourself and *thinking is the starting line.*

You have to find ways that work for you to keep yourself *positive* as it will carry through all of your communication into your actions. Being positive sounds like; *'She/he is really positive and a pleasure to be with.'*

You might even learn to like yourself a little more by concentrating on positive thoughts and keeping the 'can't' out of any conversations you are having with yourself.

Positive thoughts set the stage for how you speak to others and those listening can easily tell when someone is *positive* or negative. There are some 'buzz' words that are strong indicators of how a person is thinking. 'Can't' is at the top of the negative list along with maybe, absolutely, pessimistic, stupid, idiot, worried, etc. On the positive side we can start with 'can', probably, optimistic, hopefully, etc. You can develop your own list and remember, we are talking about *how you think* about your conversations with yourself that will filter into conversations with others. As Will Schultz, a faculty member at Harvard points out, *"my relationship with others depends largely on how I feel about myself."* [3] If you can think about things in a *positive* way, it really is time to give yourself a break; you *'probably are worth writing home about'*

Speaking

'Put your mind in gear before you put your mouth in motion.' I do not know where this came from, but maybe it should read 'Put your mind in *positive* gear before putting your mouth in motion.' Conversations with yourself can be difficult, but you really shouldn't punish yourself for your thoughts, no one else heard them. Once you start *speaking* your thoughts you become accountable for what you say. Thinking positively will certainly help you to keep what you say *positive,* but there will be times when the speed of your mind gets the mouth in motion too quickly not to say something in the wrong way. I really do not like the saying; *"You never get a second chance to make a first impression",* and I changed my version to read; *'You <u>always</u> get a second chance to make a first impression.'* Think of the times you have not liked someone when you first met them and then decided 'he's not so bad', or 'she is really pretty good at what she does.'

First impressions are being made all the time and usually through how the person is speaking. If that mouth of yours gets into motion before the positive gear in your brain is engaged, stop, correct what you said in a more positive way and apologize, if necessary, for what you said. That's the end of it, and if it takes you some time to realize you have made a bad impression, don't quit, go back and correct what you have done as soon as you can. People want to deal with *positive people* and those who can admit their mistakes. You should always be looking for ways to make conversations *positive* and you should always speak knowing you are making a first impression. First impressions do not last as long as some people think. In our crazy social media world with all the information flying about, you can be sure most people don't even remember whom they have met in a day, never mind their first impression of the person. ***You always get a second chance to make a first impression, period.*** It is always a good idea to consider all meetings where you are talking to people as ***'first impression'*** meetings. What you say and how you say it will be judged by those listening and you should always keep your guard up and remain as ***positive*** as possible.

Once in a while you will run into someone who is not positive and who you can't turn positive, and in that instance you should practice ***KYMS***, as nothing will be gained by continuing with the conversation. In some situations, ***'keeping your mouth shut'*** may be a really good ***'first impression'.*** Remember it worked for me when I went to the indoctrination meeting as a new owner of a company. (Chapter on Discipline)

Another big part of positive speaking is ***'mindful listening'.*** People can tell, by how you respond if you are listening and, if you are not, that can make all the positive words you use be negative in their mind. What you say and how you say it is being filtered by the ***radar*** of the person receiving your words and actions. Using your own ***radar and Emotional EQ*** to read the person you are talking to goes a long way in having both sides see the conversation as ***positive.*** It also will help you to deal with people the way they want to be dealt with. Always remember with whom you are speaking, ***'their way, not yours'.***

There will be times when what has to be said cannot be done in a positive way for both sides. 'You really screwed up' really doesn't sound positive to the person receiving the news, but there are ways to soften bad news and make sure the recipient hears and understands the message and does not end up devastated by what was said. I always tell people to make the bad news be about 5% of the total conversation and put it somewhere in the middle of the conversation. When you have to reprimand someone, it is usually for a part of what they have done and they probably did some of the task the right way. Use your ***Emotional EQ and radar*** to read the person, get your point across, and make the person believe they are as good as you know they can be. If you have people you don't think this way about, change the people. Remember it is your job to have the right people on the right seat in the bus and to help them turn their knowledge and skills into strengths for the team. Turning a negative into a positive by using your positive communication strengths and treating people with the utmost of respect will go a long way to making you a good leader.

Communicating with people through ***'speaking'*** has to done in a consistent or ***disciplined*** way to be sure the message you have is received by all the same way. One thing I have found that helps me to keep the conversation ***positive and consistent*** is to honestly try to like the person or persons I am talking with. I want them to like me and hear what I am saying and believe that if you want someone to like you, like them.

Follow the same routine

An example of ***consistency*** in speaking with people can be seen using the discipline I created for my presentations to the various offices in my region, that I describe in the Chapter on ***Discipline***. As described, my company had a strong discipline the included four basic value disciplines; safety, quality, financials, and people. Whenever I spoke at one of the offices, my presentation would follow the same routine. I would always start with a ***'safety minute'*** that would be a short story about some safety issue that was important to that particular office. Sometimes I would ask a member of the office to do the *'safety minute'*, but not without asking them first. Then I would continue with *'safety'*, tell them how many accidents we had and how that matched up to our plan. Then I would open the conversation to ideas on how to improve. Next I would go to *'quality'*, talk about our client surveys, compare that to our plan and again, open the floor to specifics on where we did well and where we did poorly, always trying to discuss the true facts and how to improve in a constructive manner. People always have to know they can talk about the bad without any fear of repercussion. The *'financials'* were next with comparing our billable hours to our plan with open discussion on how to get back on track, or if necessary, revising our plan for unforeseen problems that I would bring to my management.

My idea throughout all of these discussions was to keep each member of a particular office informed as to how we were all doing in accordance with our commitment to the company. The meetings would conclude with a discussion on *'people'* and how we were doing there. I always tried to start this discussion on a *personal* note, wanting to know of any new additions to families, engagements, or weddings. Sometimes we would discuss a local charitable event our people were part of and what the company could do to help. It was really important to get the point across at all times that *'people'* were the *most important part of everything we did* and the real *value* of a company that sold engineering services. Throughout these discussions we would discuss how many people, and especially key people, we lost over a period of time and we would measure that against our plan. We would also open the discussion to any problems and needs to augment staff or send work to other offices. All of this was done in an open forum with all staff members in attendance. The key point here is that any presentation I made followed the same routine and format for all offices. You have to develop **'routines'** or **'disciplines'** that you follow closely if you want to be consistent. Being **consistent** will help those you lead get to know and understand who you are and what you want to accomplish in your leadership. This is a big part of a successful **Leadership Discipline**. I still use the same four ingredients for my own company and my life discipline; **'safety, quality, financials, and people'.** Those four words highlight my business card.

The whole idea of speaking in a **consistent and positive** way should not be left at the office if you really want to develop communication as one of your **'disciplined talents'** and strengths. Take the idea home and practice it with your family and friends. You will have to change your approach and words for the different age groups in your family; you wouldn't say something the same way to your ten year old daughter than you would to your mother. Let them know you are practicing on them. See if it doesn't change, in a **positive** way, how you think about them and how they perceive you. And whatever you do, always, always, always, **leave your ego in your shoe** during any conversation. There is one thing you can always be sure of and that is; you are never **absolutely** correct, you're only **probably** correct.

Plain Talk

I want to mention a method of communication I learned a while ago called **'Plain Talk'.** Sometimes when you really need to get a point across, mostly negative, but sometimes positive it may help to tell the person or persons you are speaking with that you are going to use **'Plain Talk'** to tell them something. As I said it is usually negative and what you want to do is get the problem **out in the open** in plain, simple,

English. You don't want to hurt anyone's feelings or in any way be prejudiced toward any group, but you just have to say something that all people may not like. When and if you use this, make sure you tell them what I just told you about feelings, prejudice, etc. and let them know that after you have said what you need to say, they can comment, disagree, or whatever. The reason for using *'Plain Talk'* is to get a sensitive subject on the table without any sugar coating or concerns for hurting someone's feelings or cultures. It is not meant as the last word on the subject, it's only to open a conversation to explore the facts and get other people's input on a bothersome or troubling subject.

An example of *'Plain Talk'* that may be of help to you in understanding how and when to use it involves my time as a public official. I served as a member of the Executive Board of a community for two terms or six years. George Washington was correct, all elected officials should serve two terms maximum, but that's just one of my pet peeves, so on with the example. As the appointing authority of all employees, we had been asked by our Personnel Board to support an article in Town Meeting that would make a change in the vacation policy for all town employees. This change would alter when the town employees would be eligible for their vacation time and in short would have them wait until a year from their actual starting date of employment before taking any vacation. The present policy was that they could start taking vacation days after the first January 1 of their employment. For those employees affected, this would mean about a six month wait on their full vacation as most start dates of employment occur at the beginning of the fiscal (not physical-another pet peeve) year, July 1.

The meeting with our Personnel Board was held in the executive chamber of the town hall that held about eighty people at best. There were about two hundred town employees at the meeting to object to the change in policy. The Personnel Board made their recommendation and it was easy to see that my four colleagues on the Board were in agreement with the Personnel Board. After some really heated debate from both sides and statements by my other Board members I realized, even though I was in the minority, I had to speak. Emotions were really high in the room and throughout the building. Employees really value their vacation time, especially in the spring of the year with school vacations. It was clear that the other members of my Board were comfortable with the Personnel Boards' action and there was not a lot of '*mindful listening*' going on before I spoke.

My statement was a good example of *'Plain Talk'*. I started by saying "some may not like what I am going to say" (my warning of 'plain talk) my next statement; "I want to apologize to the town employees for even considering such a useless change to the employment policy". I said what I believed had to be said by someone. The only thing the change in policy would accomplish was to upset the plans of the town employees on vacations they had planned during school vacation for their kids. It didn't save the town money, it didn't change how much vacation they earned, it was just a collective bargaining threat to the employees and most in attendance knew that and just didn't want to bring it up.

As I thought about what to say, I couldn't find a way to be positive to all in the room. I knew going against the other four members of my board would not be the best thing for me politically as I was the last member to join the Board and still was in the 'earning respect' stage of my tenure. I also had a brother who was a police officer in the town, whose vacation would not be affected no matter what the outcome of the Town Meeting action, but I would be seen as pandering to town employees by the other board members and the Personnel Board. The decision to say what I said in apologizing came from my heart and had nothing to do with my brother or pandering to town employees. ***I said what I believed had to be said in plain simple English*** as no one was talking about or using ***radar or Emotional EQ*** at the time to soften statements because of others feelings. This meeting took place around 1980 before I, and many others, had any idea of a good ***Leadership Discipline that included considering others feelings in the speaking part of communication.***

As the town employees spoke after my statement, their emotion was more positively directed at the consequences of the proposed change and not to the personalities of their opponents. I like to think my statement let them know someone on the board was listening to their side of the situation. My board was forced to listen to what they had to say and understand their plight *(mindful listening)* My *'Plain Talk'* or apology had broken through the problem of what no one wanted to hear, the other side of the argument. We continued to listen to both sides and in the end, one vote did change and the vote was 3 to 2 to sponsor the article before Town Meeting. I took a lot of criticism from those on my Board, the Personnel Board, and other elected officials. When it got to Town Meeting, whose members are people who work and have vacations, the criticism turned completely around and the article failed by almost a unanimous vote and the policy remained the same.

This is a long story to give you some ideas on how to use *'Plain Talk'* effectively. Subjects where it is effective are usually emotional or controversial and you will probably not be able to please everyone involved. You have to think through what you are going to say and what you want to accomplish, and you may not always be correct in what you do, and it can backfire. In the example above, I had to act quickly and you may be faced with the same situation. Sometimes something just has to be said in **plain English** without considering all the consequences.

Writing

You need to write as clearly, or even clearer, than you speak. You do have an advantage here; you always have the opportunity to change what you write before you send the E-mail, note, letter or better still, the text from your phone. When speaking, the speed of the mind sometimes doesn't allow for good editing. To be a really good communicator you need to have a passion to bring your ideas to life and to make them exciting. You want people to retain what you say and value your information. When speaking or writing you want to use the perfect phrase by using dramatic words and powerful word combinations.

Communication is your best tool in leading people and inspiring them to act. It is important that you continually use the editing tool when writing to be sure you have said what you want to say without any **'emotional cloud'** or ego. This is especially true when **texting** as this form of communication is almost as fast as talking and can be very impersonal, especially to those receiving the text. It is best to complete the written document and then leave it for a while and then go back, read it again, and make any edits that will make it better, and then send it. The odds are you will have some changes before the final version is sent. When texting this is hard to do, but you should remember that what you text is a document that will last and can be retrieved if necessary. You should also remember that **texting usually takes place when you are multitasking and you are not being as consciously involved as if you were actually writing a document. You are basically trying to write at the speed of your mind. This is not good.** Texting is a good place to practice all of your *'positive'* communication skills and keep the negative for a more well thought out document or conversation.

Always remember to **write** the way those receiving the document will want to read and receive the message. Use their style, not yours and read and listen to what you have written. There is never a reason to offend anyone with what you write, and **remember it is much harder to take back the written word than the spoken word.** Words have a lot of meaning to each of us and those meanings are not always the same for all of us, especially within the diverse society we have become. Understanding different cultures and being able to effectively communicate with them requires good **radar and Emotional EQ talents and strengths.** Knowing your audience can be a task in itself. Trying to write something that all will understand in the same way can be really difficult. Some pointers may include: keeping the message short, not covering too many subjects, being consistent with words and phrases, making sure those receiving the message know they can call you for a spoken clarification if necessary.

You may also want to use the *'story telling trick'* to get a point across when writing. People sometimes understand something better if they see it in the form of an example or event that they can relate to. You have *'probably'* noticed throughout this book that I sometimes accentuate my writing with thoughts that I have while I am writing. My hope in doing this is to show you some emotional input into what I am trying to get across to you in this book. **Straightforward, honest, positive thoughts go a long way in making a point in a written document.** You should be careful in how you use it, but not afraid to try it at some point. It is also important in both the spoken or written word to be *'mindful of the diversity'* of our society. Think of how many ways you would have to say a simple 'hello' if you wanted to speak to all cultures in our society. Making an *'off the cuff'* comment about any culture is *'probably'* going to offend someone if you are not really careful in choosing your words.

Again, always remember that *'all people are really important'* and have equal status. I always think of the quote on immigration by G.W. Bush that says: *"All immigrants make America more American."* Can you imagine life without *'pizza'* from the Italians, *'potatoes'* from the Irish, *'taco's'* from the Hispanic's, or *'peanuts'* from the Africans'. (Some would say peanuts came from Brazil, but they went through Africa on their way to the US), and what about *'Chinese Food'* and all the other really quality things we get from our immigrants? We are lucky to live in such a *'diverse and free'* society and we should always remember the importance of each and every one, as at one time *we were all immigrants.*

Actions

Your *actions* are a large part of your *communication discipline* and *talent.* How you sit, stand, hold your arms and hands when you speak are very important to how you will be received. When working with a group you want to be consistent by letting them know your routine for communicating with people. They should know that you will always be: open to hearing what they think, wanting to hear the *'bad news' without reprisal,* knowing you are *'probably'* and not absolutely correct, and that their ideas matter and have standing with you. Although most of this will be accomplished in what you say, your actions have to complement your words. If you tell them you are open to their ideas, you should demonstrate the same with your actions; a smile, or arm gesture that welcomes their thoughts. Asking to hear the 'bad news' without reprisal won't be seen in a *positive* way if the look on your face is menacing; better to smile and make some positive facial gesture, and maybe pause a little to let them know you really mean what you say. It is also important to be **consistent** in your delivery so those in attendance can learn to read you through your actions. If you can accomplish this type of attitude with those you communicate with on a regular basis through your actions and routines when speaking or writing, then you will be seen as having a successful **communications discipline** that people will come to respect.

When you are talking to people, pausing at the right time can be an important action as it indicates you want feedback or comments. Be sure to take any feedback offered by listening closely and taking notes if necessary. Asking questions during conversations is also a good way to get the discussion and ideas flowing. It shows your openness, or to use, the 'new' more powerful word, **'transparency'**. In today's 'social media world' there are phrases and actions that have powerful meanings. Understanding this new 'lingo' will help you to develop the good quality of **diversity** in communicating with people and understanding how others may relate to what you are saying or writing. You should also demonstrate your **mindful listening** skills in a way obvious to all. You may choose to repeat something that someone has said or actually ask the person to elaborate on their point. Be consistent and genuine with what you do and how you do it. You want to establish your own **discipline** through the actions you use when communicating. Consistency in words and actions will help you to effectively and continually communicate your **Leadership Discipline**. Make sure you always give a subject all the time necessary so that all understand and digest what it is you are trying to get across. You have to get beyond the **'headlines'** if you want people to really understand your point. You should never rush through a topic that you completely understand, thinking that everyone else has the same understanding as you. Remember, you're only *'probably'* right and others may see the same point in a different way.

Mindful Listening

Some say *'you have two ears and one mouth'* to demonstrate how important listening is in communication. That is probably truer now than ever before with all the social media *'dribble'* that takes place on every subject known to man. The big trick in understanding what is worth while is the filter you use to cull out the crap, and the only way to get the filter right is to be a *good listener*. Once again, listening starts with your own thought process and the confidence you have in yourself and your *talents.* If you honestly believe you *'probably'* are really good at something then hearing another point of view on that subject will not threaten your belief and you can be open to changes in what you believe. Being 'absolutely' sure of yourself is like a wall to *mindful listening*, as your *ego* gets into the act, and God forbid someone attacks your ego. When you learn to honestly respect your *'talents'* and how to navigate around some of your weaknesses you will see how much you can learn from really listening to other points of view.

The best example I can share with you on respecting and learning from others is the conversations with my wife. First of all, you have to understand that she is a lot smarter than me, and I have a much larger ego. We also have different political positions and personalities; she is quiet, reserved and I am much the opposite. It took years for me to really apply *mindful listening* to a lot of our conversations. I would usually have developed my opinion of something and then would ask her what she thought. She, of course, would have her own undeveloped opinion and state it in a much different way than my mind had developed what I was asking her about. A lot of times her ideas were really worth hearing and because her thought process was a lot different than mine, there was a wall blocking what I would hear. The first thing I had to do was believe in the word *'probably'*. Thinking that my ideas were *'probably'* right got rid of the *ego* problem and gave my ideas standing in the conversation that could be changed. The next thing was to appreciate that she had a much different thought process and used more subtle words and actions to explain her position. I had to *put my expectations aside* and hear what she was saying in accordance *with her expectations*. And last, but not least, I had to learn to slow down to her pace and let her develop her position in her own way. Usually when you ask someone their opinion you have already done a lot of thinking about the subject and formed you own opinion. The person you are seeking the opinion from has *'probably'* not done as much thinking on the subject and needs time to gather their thoughts and put them into words, so *slow down* and give them the time they need. I still ask her opinion on many subjects and enjoy listening to her ideas much more now that I have disciplined myself on how to have a meaningful conversation with *mindful listening*.

As I have said, take some of your knowledge and skills home to practice, a friendly face and attitude from someone you care about can go a long way in further *developing your strengths*. Oh, and I still disagree with her on a lot of subjects, but I have learned to respect what she believes and that has been very helpful in my ability to honestly listen to the opinion of others. All people have something to contribute; all you have to do is listen.

I hope this chapter on *Communication* helps you to understand how important it is to be positive in *'thinking, speaking, writing, actions, and listening'*. I hope you also see how important it is to be able to communicate *'Your Leadership Discipline'* to those you work with and those you care about in your life.

There are *four agreements* from a book with the same name that provide some good guidance for communicating in a consistent and meaningful way: *"be impeccable with your word, don't take anything personally, don't make assumptions, and always do your best."*[4] These agreements certainly are directed at more than how you communicate; they represent your good, solid, character and how you should deal with others. The book they are quoted from, *"The Four Agreements"*, is well worth reading as it explains the importance of each of the *agreements* and helps you learn the importance of *consistency*, or *discipline,* with honesty, controlling your ego, respecting the thoughts of others, and always doing your best. Much of what we have discussed throughout this book.

Chapter 7
THE 'BEGINNING' AT 'THE END'

This is 'the beginning' and it is 'at the end'. So what does that mean: it's simple, it is time to begin to use *'Your Leadership Discipline'* and it's at the end of the book. Sometimes the most excitement is when the effort is completed, and other times it is when you are just starting. Lucky you, we have both here; you completed the book and can now start to develop, learn, and use *your* new *'Leadership Disciplines'*. Finally, you can admit to the *talents* you *probably* have and start to use the *routines* that will become the *disciplines* you need to *communicate* your *talents* and *strengths* to make life and work a lot better for you and those you come in contact with on a daily basis.

Two things we want to do here is to complete a quick review of what I hoped you would learn by reading this book and the associated material suggested and, using the documentation you collected throughout your work, to develop a written version of *'Your Leadership Disciplines'*.

The Quick Review

A quick summary of what happened in this book and hopefully what you *learned* begins with the following;

How the world is changing

Why talents are so important in life and work leadership

How to take the 'Shortcut' in learning and understanding all of this

Who you *honestly* are,

What your *talents probably* are

How to create *routines* and *disciplines* to use your *talents*

How to *communicate* your *talents* to others.

Hopefully, you also learned the *positive* use of the word *probably*, how to keep *your ego in your shoe*, when to use *KYMS,* and ways to keep *positive* thoughts, words, and actions in all you do in life. It would also help if you became somewhat *suspicious* of the *facts or fiction* promoted by social media, the use of *radar* in respecting all people's thoughts and actions and when to use *plain talk* to get a sensitive topic on the table without it being considered a personal insult. Also included should be a good understanding of *diversity* in all that we do and the *'absolute'* statement that *'all people matter'*.

Those of us brought up in the US or other Western cultures should always remember the *advantage* of being educated in a *free society*. It's that type of society that influences educational systems and directs us to concentrate on a *'talent based meritocracy'* rather than an *'exam based meritocracy'* and to use our creativity, curiosity, sense of adventure, imagination, and ambition in fully developing our talents and skills. This same *advantage* of a *free society* also provides us with the social skills needed to learn, acknowledge, and value "*feelings in ourselves and others* and to be able to respond to those *feelings* effectively, applying the information and energy of *emotions* in our daily life and work."[1] In short, being brought up in a free society provides advantages in caring about the *diversity* within our society, realizing the importance of all *people*, and being better prepared to *lead others and ourselves effectively.*

I also hope you had some fun in learning all of this and consider yourself better off and on your way to making the jump from *management to leadership* at work. And I hope you realize the importance of having a *life leadership discipline* and how important that is to all of us having a better America and a better world. Throughout the book I have used stories to make a point on a particular *talent* or *discipline,* and I hope there was some benefit for you in those as well. A good self evaluation of life is the stories we tell to others about what we did and what we wanted to do. Hopefully this book will help you create some really *good stories* of a positive life. Those *stories* will help you understand yourself and your *talents and skills* as the more you tell them the more you will understand *your recurring thoughts, feelings and behavior.*

I was lucky as a kid to have met John Kennedy when I was about fifteen. It was on Cape Cod just before his run for President and we got to meet him three or four times while his wife took water skiing lessons on the beach where we all hung out. One of my friends' brothers was the instructor and some of us would help to show Mrs. Kennedy how to do certain things on the water skis. It made us all feel great when he recognized us at an event where we went to see him on his return to the Cape after he announced he would run for President. *'Boy, were we special'.* Throughout my life I have always held on to that honor and imagined myself as being *'significant'* and able to make a difference in life. I don't think all of my considering myself to be *'significant'* came from meeting a really great guy who would become the President at a young age, but I do believe it had something to do with one of my strengths in the StrengthsFinder being *"Significance"*. As I said before, your *life stories* help to define you as a person and usually are made up of your *talents and strengths.* I can't imagine how many times I have told this story, but you can be sure that each time made me feel *significant* and really good, and helped me to get my point across in a way I felt really comfortable with.

When President Obama was inaugurated I watched on television as many high school bands marched past the President's reviewing stand. The kids had been told to look straight ahead, not at the President, but as they marched past their necks would strain trying to put their heads in a position to see the President without being obvious. How appropriate for a kid who met a popular President, and one of his heroes, to see a bunch of black kids see and perform for another popular President and I'm sure one of their heroes. I hope these kids will carry that honor with them and realize that what they accomplish in life is *significant* and worth *'writing home about'*. Our country and world is changing and a lot for the better. I like to tell this story when I want people to know how the *world is changing for the better*, or when I want to drive home the point of *diversity in our society* and how *all lives matter.* You can read more about my meeting JFK and the black kids performing for President Obama in the story "Pride and Imagination" found in "The Stories" at the end of the book. This story helps to drive home the point of how important things we experience at a young age can be to us throughout life.

I know you will have a story that makes you feel *significant* and that how you lead in life *using your talents* will affect others in a positive way. Remember when you write down **Your Leadership Discipline,** that **you are something to write home about,** and your **life stories** will describe you as you make a difference to the many that are watching you.

Continuing on with the review, there are some questions for you to answer to do a self evaluation of just what you did learn from the book. They are arranged in accordance with the chapters as written. Hopefully, you will be able to answer them without much thought and that will help you in going forward with **'Creating Your Leadership Discipline'.** You can consider this a test if you want, but it is really meant to have you discover where some holes in your reading retention may be so that you can go back and fill in any information on answers you consider important.

You might want to jot down answers to some of the questions and consider this an outline for your **Leadership Discipline**. At any rate, answering the questions should be a fun way of summarizing the book and what I hoped you would learn.

Prologue
How important are talents in a talent based meritocracy?
Can we test for curiosity, creativity, a sense of adventure and ambition?
Is America declining, or is the rest of the world rising?
Do you really want to create a **leadership discipline** for yourself?

Chapter 1 The Short Cut
Did you learn that this book can be used as a **'short cut'** to learning what your talents are and how to create a discipline for them?
Did you find that you really do not have to read an entire book to get the information you need if someone tells you what you need to know?
Did the review of the Chapters help you to understand the book?

Do you think taking the *'short cut'* is an effective way to get started on learning what your talents are and how to create a discipline to use them productively?

Who founded Thayer Academy?

How high was Butchie's Berlin wall?

What was the 'fat' kids name?

Chapter 2 *The Changing World*

Is the United States still a world leader?

Is the 'Rising of the Rest' a failure of the US?

When did the US become the leader and dominate global economics?

What has been the economic growth rate of the nations taking the lead?

Where are these nations?

Where is the tallest building in the world?

Where is the largest shopping mall?

What has the US's average economic growth rate been in the last ten years?

Has the average family GDP in the US gone up considerably lately?

How many terms should any US Politician serve?

How many people died due to the Second World War?

How many Jews were killed in the Second World War?

How many people died because of the attack on 9/11?

In today's world what do we have to fear most?

Is today's world as scary as the world was during World War II?

How much *opportunity* is there in the technical changes taking place today?

Are there new *leadership opportunities* in science, medicine and business?

At what levels do these opportunities in leadership exist?

What was the first success of the telephone?

Who started the internet and when?

Does *social media* always tell the truth?

What group of people in the US has the most unused **potential to lead others**?

What group of people in the US has been **most prejudiced against** in leadership positions?

What is a **Renaissance Person**?

What **prejudices** are **ingrained** in our culture?

Will there be **changes** in the future?

How will **humans add value** to our society?

Chapter 3 Understanding Who You Are

What do people usually answer when asked what their **talents** are?

What is a talent?

What is the D-I-S-C process?

What is a 360 evaluation?

Should we value **feelings** of others in business decisions?

What is Emotional EQ?

Is the heart just a pump, or does it do more with the mind?

How did you rank yourself in curiosity, communication, Emotional IQ and imagination?

Are you something to **write home about**?

What were your test results?

Do you have to believe in yourself to be a good leader?

Chapter 4 Talents

Are you **'probably'** good at something or are you absolutely sure you are good at something?

Do you know **who you are** yet?

What would **you write** to describe **you** to someone else?

What is the best advantage those of us in the US have to become leaders?

How many talents are there?

Where does a talent begin?

What is a *four lane highway talent*?

How about a *dirt road talent*?

How do you discover your talents?

What is an *intuitive talent*?

What are *reasoning or learned skills*?

Are *gut feelings* something you should use to help make decisions?

What are *recurring patterns of thought, feeling, or behavior?*

What are some *emotional talents?*

What is *Radar?*

Did you *document* your talents?

What did the Disney character say about thinking, or talking about yourself?

Chapter 5 Discipline

What does *KYMS* stand for?

Does a *discipline* start with a *simple routine*?

Who won the 2000 presidential election?

What are companies *Value Disciplines*? (FedEx, Airborne, Wall-Mart)

Can people develop *value discipline* for using their *talents*?

What are some *basic ingredients* for *a leadership discipline*?

What does using the word *probably* help you do?

Can you *practice* your talents?

What shot, *his best, or his worst*, does Tiger Woods *practice* the most?

How many miles did the author walk as an average each year?

How important is *consistency* to a *leadership discipline?*

How about *persistence?*

Do *emotions* play a part in using your *talents* in leading others?

How important is *thinking* in *talking* and *doing*?

What is the best way for the author to *commit to something*?

Is there a way to *stop worrying?*

Chapter 6 Communication

What is the one *thing to be* when you are communicating with someone?

What do you need to *accentuate* while communicating?

What do you need to *eliminate* while communicating?

Is the first action you take when communicating *talking?*

Are you right if you think *you can?*

Are you right if you think *you can't?*

Can you put *worry aside* and think positive thoughts?

Does how you think about *yourself* affect how you think about others?

When do you get a *second chance* to make a first impression?

Does another person's *radar* effect how they hear what you are saying?

What *four subjects* did the authors *work discipline* include?

What is *plain talk*, and when should you use it?

Can plain talk be used to get beyond the emotional aspects of a subject?

Should you *announce* to your audience that you are going to use *plain talk?*

What is a big advantage to *writing* something when *communicating?*

Is there a *disadvantage* to writing something when *communicating?*

Should you be careful when communicating by *texting?*

Is it good to be able to *tell stories* when communicating?

Does your *demeanor* when speaking have any effect on how you are received?

What is *mindful listening?*

Is *listening* important when *communicating?*

Can you *practice and improve* your communication *talents and skills?*

The Stories

What did you learn about using *'The Shortcut'?*

Where did the author rank himself with the others walking to school?

How *big* are things to a *small* kid?

Do problems as a kid tend to get *smaller* as you grow up?

Is it important to remember *stories* that happened to you as a kid?

What *talents* did Butchie probably start to learn on the shortcut?

How did *Azel Road* impact the author?

What *'4 lane highway talent'* of the author had its birth on *Azel Road*?

Do your *parents* have any influence in you developing your *talents?*

Do your *siblings* have any influence in you developing your *talents?*

How do *important people* in your life at a *young age* effect the development of your *talents?*

How important is *KYMS* to the author?

Is *'keeping your mouth shut'* a talent or a discipline?

Should the CEO have practiced *KYMS* when he used the word *nonsensical?*

Is *mindful listening* important in a conversation?

Is writing *KYMS* on the top of each note page a simple routine?

How important is the use of the word *'probably'* in describing what you think is a fact?

Are you *'absolutely'* correct or *'probably'* correct?

What *religion* does the author practice?

How do you *'keep your ego in your shoe'* and out of conversations?

What's a good way to learn to use *'probably'* in conversations?

Is the use of *'maybe'* the same as the use of **'probably'**?

When is it appropriate to use *'plain talk'* in a discussion?

Has social media gone overboard with *'political correctness?'*

Should you announce that you are using *'plain talk'* or just say what you want without regard to being accused of being insulting?

How important is it to respect *all* in a conversation?

What's a good definition of *'diversity'*?

Was the author's use of *'plain talk'* during his government meeting received *'positively'* by all in attendance?

Is there a risk to using *'plain talk'*?

What role did meeting *JFK* play in helping to develop the author's *talents?*

Are young minds more apt to be influenced with information than older minds?

How many times do you think the author told the *JFK* story?

Do you think an event like meeting a President at a young age can help to develop a *Significance Strength?*

Can you water ski on one ski?

How about the *black kids* getting to see *President Obama* on his inauguration day, will they remember that day?

Is our world changing for the better now that we have, or at least tried, to end an *ingrained prejudice?*

Do you think the kids had sore necks? Or that they cared?

Is it great that some *black kids* got to have the same feeling of *Significance* as a *white kid* and it only took *48 years?*

Why did it take so long?

Do *ingrained prejudices* have a place in our society?

Is it time for *diversity* and *equality for all people* in our society?

Can you write a *discipline, or simple routine* to practice *honest diversity* in your *leadership disciplines?*

The Beginning

Now that the test is over, and I hope you passed with flying colors, its time to do one more thing; *'The Beginning'*. You should start this by gathering all your notes on talents, strengths, knowledge, discipline, communication, etc. and all that you documented. This should be short and sweet and include a short, simple list of your various types of *talents,* including *innate and intuitive,* as well as *reasoning or learned skills,* some of the *routines or disciplines* you have created to consistently use your talents and some ideas on how to practice. Remember; practice your best talents the most. You can also do this in two sections: those *talents* and *disciplines* for your *life leadership discipline* and then add in the *talents* and *value disciplines* for your *work leadership discipline*.

This document will become *Your Leadership Discipline* and with enough practice, help you succeed in both work and life. Try writing it as a short story about where you want you life to go, both at work and in your community. You should also consider a time line on where you want to be in say five years. There will still be changes you have to accommodate, but a five year look ahead is a good place to start. While you are putting these leadership disciplines together, please don't forget your *significant stories* and what it is that people *will want to write home about you*. Throughout your life, you will continue to realize that *your stories* and the *stories of others that stick with you* will be the true explanation of your *talents,* and what you do well. The *stories* I have told you in this book contain many of my *4 lane highway talents*, and I know yours will do the same.

Now lets get on it and put together your plan, and remember, *plan your work and work your plan*. Also remember that you are creating ideas on what your talents are and how to use them to your benefit. This document is for your use, so don't get all caught up in how well it is written, make it work for you. A lot of what you have learned about yourself will not have to be written down and as you go forward, more and more of what you are doing will become almost automatic in your thinking. Believe me, having a *Leadership Discipline* will become a *talent* in itself.

YOUR LEADERSHIP DISCIPLINE

In an effort to keep this simple, I thought a template might help you to fill in the blanks and get on with documenting all that should go into your *Leadership Discipline*. I will use some of my own information in this template and then leave blanks for your information. Remember a short story about yourself and what you want to accomplish in the next five years is a good place to start. You can go back to "Break All The Rules", the chapter on "Skills Knowledge and Talents" and "Now Discover Your Strengths" the "StrengthsFinder" to help you choose your five or so *'4 lane highway talents'*. You can also look at "The Discipline of Market Leaders" to refresh yourself on *'value disciplines'* for the five or so *disciplines* you want to develop to *communicate and practice your talents.* Remember to include the different types of talents, especially the *innate* talents, *(natural abilities or aptitude)* and *intuitive talents* that include *(emotion and feelings).*

Life Leadership Discipline
Talents
The authors'
Empathy, significance, numerical, gestalt, honesty, spiritual awareness, communication, and imagination.
(these examples include*; innate talents* (numerical, gestalt, honesty) they include *intuitive talents* (empathy, significance, imagination)

and they include ***knowledge and skills*** (spiritual awareness and communication)

Now list yours;

_____   _____   _____   _____

Disciplines
The authors'
Probably, KYMS, thinking positively, simple routines, documentation, radar, mindful thinking and listening.
(I use probably, KYMS and thinking positively with spiritual awareness and communication talents. I use simple routines and documentation for my numerical and gestalt talents, and I use radar and mindful thinking and listening for honesty and communication talents).

Now list yours;

_____   _____   _____   _____

Practice Routines
The authors'
Mindfulness, telling and writing stories, learning and experimenting, imagining the impossible, documentation
(When I need to get more ***positive in thinking***, I will use mindfulness or meditation as practice. I can tell or write a story
to practice ***communication***. I might imagine the impossible for working on my ***radar*** talent, and I document everything).

Now list yours;

_____   _____   _____   _____

<u>Work Leadership Discipline</u>

Added responsibilities, or ***value disciplines***, for specific leadership positions;

The authors'

Safety, Quality, Financials, People, Engineering skills, Political skills
(***Value disciplines*** are specific to your work responsibilities and usually included your knowledge and skills. You will use all of your talents to communicate these and ***consistency*** in presentation will become a good ***discipline*** to develop).

Now list yours;

_____ _____ _____ _____

Now that you have collected all your documentation and recorded what you think your talents and disciplines ***probably*** are, it is time to start practicing what you preach. Take each talent and see if you can't practice at least telling someone what you think it ***'probably'*** is and how you would use it in life and work. It is best to start with someone you trust and maybe to start at home where people know what you are reading and trying to accomplish. Starting with someone you know is the beginning of your discipline. When you try something new, try it with someone who knows you. Remember, people do not really know what their talents are, never mind what someone may be doing in trying to learn their ***talents*** and put together a ***discipline*** to use them properly.

As an example, if one of your ***talents*** is ***communication,*** and I hope it is, you can start with a ***conversation*** that you have really ***thought through*** and see if your partner notices any difference in your approach. You can set up a simple routine to do this that would include the following; ***think*** about what you want to say, ***say it to your partner*** in a *positive* way watching your *demeanor*, listen in a *mindful* way to any comments, and then *document* what you did and what you learned. The documentation can just be a short note on when you did it and how you think you did. It does help to be able to easily see your documentation sheet, so if you can hang a calendar on a wall and make notes on a daily basis, you will remember what you have accomplished and hopefully see progress. I like to use a dry erase board that I can change on a monthly basis, and my notes are usually one or two words that fit on a monthly calendar layout. As you get into this you will find it simple to see progress or that you are not doing anything to go forward.

Recently I attended a meditation course that required daily meditation and mindfulness thinking. When I did what the course required, the calendar got a big M, when I cheated a bit it got a small m or m- and when I did nothing it got a big 0. It really is important to document what ever you are doing, even if you erase it after the month.

As you practice learning your *talents and disciplines,* try to start with one or two and develop *routines* and then *document* your progress. You can't do it all at once and once you feel comfortable with one, you can start another. Hopefully, as you learn it will become automatic for you to use your *talents* and *disciplines* as part of your regular *daily routines*.

A simple routine that may help you stay on course in *Creating Your Leadership Discipline* is to work at doing something *positive* that will earn you a thank you from two people before you get to work. This is a mindfulness exercise that will help you start the day on a *positive* note and keep you focused on using *Your Leadership Discipline*. After all, if two people say thank you to you, you must be doing something right.

The documentation for this will be easy. Each day you can write a 2, a 1, or a big fat 0 on your calendar.

You may want to write your first short story around ***Your Leadership Discipline,*** what you learned, what your ***talents*** are and what ***disciplines*** you plan to use to learn how to ***communicate*** your ***talents*** to those at work and in your social community. Or you may already have a ***story*** that happened in the past that illustrates one of your ***talents or disciplines***. Try writing it down and using it with a friend to explain one of your talents. A good short story can become a good work plan to follow. Telling it over and over is the way to understand ***recurring thoughts, feelings or behavior.*** It is also a way to learn, respect and use your talents, skills and routines or disciplines.

While you are writing Your Leadership Disciplines, always remember to use the book for quick reference, remembering it is a ***'shortcut'*** to what you want to learn.

I think I am done. My E-mail for this book is CYLD @ beld.net. I will try to answer any questions you may have, and ***mindfully listen*** to any criticism you many have of what I have written. I would also appreciate any of your ideas on making the book better. I do not think I would be a good 'partner' for you to try out ideas on your ***talents*** or ***disciplines*** as I do have very strong expectations of myself that would flow into criticism of anything you wrote or did.

You may not know it, but if you got to this point in the book by reading it all, ***you are already something to write home about.*** Good luck and thanks for listening.

The Stories

Life is just a bunch of ***short stories*** and following are some of mine that help to make important points about my life, my business experience, and the parts of this book that I really want you to learn. You ***probably*** have heard of, or even taken courses that use the ***'Case Study'*** method of teaching. To me, telling stories is that type of teaching. As you read through this book you will hopefully recall situations in your life that you find interesting enough to write short stories about. You may even find stories that help you get to know and understand your ***talents***, ***strengths***, and ***disciplines***. All of this goes along with my premise that you can learn your ***talents*** and develop a ***discipline*** to use them and communicate them to others, and have fun at the same time. Believe me, writing your own ***short stories*** will help you do all of the above and it will be fun. I am going to give you the titles of my stories and a short description of what I think you may learn by reading and studying them. There may be more to them than what you first learn when reading them. Think them through, consider them a ***'Case Study'***, pay attention to what I say about myself and the ***relationships*** within the story, and remember, ***thinking*** is the first step in communicating. When you develop your own stories, tell them often and get to know all you have to say in them. They will become part of who you are in a very positive way, and for goodness sake, use your ***imagination*** when thinking them through and writing them.

Now for my stories and a short take on why you should read them.

The Story	*The Short Take*
Azel Road	*Helps you to understand where Some Talents may come from*
Erin's Lighthouse's	*Details of Cultural Change and demonstration of Emotional Talents*
Pride and Imagination	*Explains Significanct as a strength and Cultural Changes*
The First Chatham A's Game	*Demonstrates how Emotional Talents sound and How people think and speak of Themselves*
Two Kids on a Plane	*Demonstrates why it is so important to stay positive with everyone*
The Flight Attendant	*Demonstrates "Always do the right thing, it doesn't have to happen"*
The Ninth Grade Dance	*Helps you to understand Talents developed at a really young age, continue throughout Life,(see Azel Road story)*
Five Women and a Really Big Little Boy	*Helps you to understand how you continue to learn from others close to you*

Azel Road

The story of ***Azel Road*** took place when I was about six years old. I lived in a nice town, was upper lower class. My father had a steady job in a ship yard and my mother worked as a part time nurse in the nursing home that was next door to my house. It was owned by a friend of my mothers' who would be like an aunt to me throughout life. ***Azel Road*** was a road about one hundred feet from my house that intersected with my street, Franklin Street. Franklin Street was a main road, a state highway of the 1950's and ***Azel Road*** was a very small street with about twenty or so houses in total. When I would go to the park, French's Common, to play, my walk to the park would require me to cross ***Azel Road.*** Not a problem as there was little traffic to worry about and the sidewalk along Franklin Street was a safe place for a six year old to walk. ***(Think about that and how things have changed. Imagine a six year old being allowed to go off to a park half mile from his home, by himself, today, I don't think so.)***

Any way, off I would go down Franklin Street, across ***Azel Road*** up to Central Avenue, turn left on Central Avenue and go to Tremont Street, cross Central Avenue and go down Tremont Street to the park. It was a dream place for a six year old: sand boxes, basketball and tennis courts, baseball fields, swings, seesaws, the works. What a place to be, and all for me and my army of friends who lived in the neighborhood. I would go there four or five times a week in the school year and every day in the summer months when there were two park instructors that arranged various playground activities for the kids of the neighborhood.

John Bergoli was the instructor for the boys and really a great guy. When I was six he was probably sixteen and had the job in the summer for two or three years as he went through high school and onto college.

He lived in the neighborhood, on Central Avenue, actually, and I would see him a lot, as I passed his house, on my way to and from the park. He was part of a large family like mine and had brothers and sisters the same age as my brothers and sisters and they all knew each other which **added to the security of a six year old going to the park by himself.**

I was very lucky growing up to live in a good neighborhood with great people who really cared for each other and their families. Much later in life, when I became a Selectman in my home town, I had the privilege to vote to appoint Ken Bergoli, John's nephew as a police officer. It was my relationship as a kid with his family that gave me the confidence that he would be a good cop, and he has always done an excellent job for the people of the town.

One day, a Saturday, as I remember, I wanted to go the park. I was home alone with my mother as my father had gone off with his friend, probably to the dog track, and my older brother Bill was nowhere to be found. My mother and father had a strained relationship as my father drank on weekends and could be abusive at times. My mother, being brought up in an upper middle class household, had really lost most of her happiness living with her situation. She had her work as a nurse that she took very seriously and her children, all of whom had left home to marry with the exception of me and Bill. Her work at the nursing home brought her close to many patients and the care, both physically and psychologically, she gave to those people at all times was exceptional. I would sometimes visit with the patients and got to know some of them and just how much they thought of my mother. They would always be telling me what *'Mae'* had done for them or how she was the only one who visited them on a special holiday to be sure they were okay, happy, and not alone. She was certainly a person who had learned to **care for** *others in a selfless manner* and put her own worries aside or as she would say "on the back burner".

On this particular Saturday my mother was home alone with her six year old 'Butchie' (me) and was somewhat content with that until Butchie asked to go to the park "for something to do". It was about two in the afternoon on a hot summer day and I remember my mother becoming really sad and saying "doesn't anyone care about being with me?" I think she actually cried a bit. After persisting, she finally said as she always would, *caring about the feelings of someone else*, "ok, go ahead, be careful crossing the streets". Off I went with a smile on my face. When I got to *Azel Road* and was just about across the street, stepping up onto the Franklin Street sidewalk, it hit me like a ton of bricks. I actually felt really sad for my mother being left home alone while everyone else was off having fun. Although I kept on going, sometimes thinking to turn back, the sadness remained with me on the walk to the park and probably dissipated after I got playing with my friends, but obviously it never went away. I know the exact spot on *Azel Road* where I had that feeling of sadness for someone else and *actually cared for their feelings, and remember, I was six years old.*

Looking back on my childhood and especially my times at the nursing home with the patients and listening and learning how someone, my mother, had cared for them, their loneliness, and well being, *I have to believe that this event on Azel Road and the thoughts of my mothers loneliness is where the 'four lane highway' in my brain, or empathy talent, had started to be carved out to become the foundation for my emotional talents.* All my life I have been able to sense and care about the emotions of others, and I believe *those talents came from my mother* as she is the one who truly sensed and cared for the emotions of others. She always put the feelings of others first and only this one time, on that hot Saturday, did she falter and care a little for herself. As I think back it was probably good for me that she did, as I was very lucky to have the mother I had and ***probably*** just as lucky to have ***Azel Road*** as a story to tell.

My suggestion to you is to look back to your childhood for your ***Azel Road*** stories. Try to remember situations with your family or close friends where ***you may have been startled or impressed with a situation that you have always remembered, and maybe even told as one of your short stories.*** Remember, ***talents begin at a really young age*** and some believe they are pretty much developed by the time you are in your mid-teens. ***'Four lane highways' are built early in life and require constant maintenance and use as they become knowledge and strengths.***

Erin's Lighthouses

(This story was written in 2006 and demonstrates how *cultural change* effects *diversity and ingrained prejudice in our society*. It shows how people are working to make America better using all *the talents of immigrants* who find themselves living in a part of America some thought would never change. It also shows the importance of all people and the hard work it takes to involve everyone. There are a lot of *emotional talents* demonstrated throughout this story.)

South Boston is a very special place to many people. There are stories about stories of how this person did this and that person did that. In my day all the stories had something to do with the Irish of Boston, because Southie is where they called home in the City of Boston. Things change, and in a recent visit to Southie, I learned just how much they are changing. My daughter Erin is a counselor in the Boston public schools. She works for Boston Medical, which is a part of B.U. and provides medical services to the City of Boston. She works closely with the other service departments of the city that try and *improve the overall outlook for the kids of Boston*. One of Erin's associates runs a program that brings art instruction to the people of South Boston. This year the project was called the *"Lighthouse Art Project"*. The idea was to have children of all ages work with the young art students at the *Artists For Humanity Center* to create Lighthouses, made of plywood that would be displayed throughout Southie. The children were allowed to develop their own theme and then the top sixty would actually paint their own lighthouse on the plywood cutouts. They also received a lot of help from some of the artists who run the Artists For Humanity Center. When Erin saw the results of the project she invited Kathy and me to the official ceremony to acknowledge all who had contributed to the project including some of the young people who had painted their own lighthouse. The event was held on West Broadway, one of the main streets, that goes through South Boston. The completed lighthouses had been displayed at light poles along West Broadway. When Kathy and I arrived it was very easy to see why Erin had invited us: the artwork was really great and the themes of the lighthouses captured the thoughts of the young artists. ***It was a way for the kids to tell people about their lives, concerns, hopes, dreams and future.*** There were all levels of artwork, some really good and some very elementary, but the stories told on the lighthouses were very clear. ***You could see the stories about stories and you could especially see the changes that are occurring in one of Boston's oldest neighborhoods.*** Our good president, George Bush said in his first inauguration speech; ***"every immigrant makes America more American"***. To me, this is one of his best comments.

In Southie, that day, Kathy and I saw how the president's quote is coming true in an area that we know really well. Kathy started her life in the projects of South Boston, just down the street from where we had gathered for the event. I have spent most of my adult life going to school and working in Boston, and have become part of the fabric of the city with most of my friendship ties being in Southie. ***Of course to Kathy and me South Boston was Irish and the stories our friends, and acquaintances told usually had some ties to the Emerald Isle.*** What we saw that very hot day in July was so much different, and at the same time, so very similar to what we knew Southie to be.

Each one of the lighthouses told it's story of what the kids saw in Southie in 2006. ***Every culture you can imagine was represented here.*** There was, of course, an ***Irish lighthouse***, showing the Irish Cross, shamrocks, and other Irish symbols. Just next to that was an ***African-American lighthouse*** where a kid had painted a portrait of himself dancing. Then there was a ***Native American lighthouse*** that reminded us who was here before we got here. There were **Puerto Rican lighthouses, Asian lighthouses** and many more that showed how Southie had changed. **There were also lighthouses that showed how Southie had not changed.** Kids expressed the frustration with life and the hopelessness that they feel every day. Expressions like "don't quit" "keep trying" "we will overcome" were written on the lighthouses. There were lighthouses that showed the effects of drugs and alcohol and other demons that kids face every day, whether it be loneliness, fear, or just plain despair with their life. And, there were lighthouses that said just the opposite; real hope, accomplishment, love of life and family, and hopeful looks into the future.

While we waited for the program to begin, Erin introduced us to one of the people responsible for the program. (Maya Rodriguez) **She was about forty-five, Puerto Rican, (I think) and just full of life and excitement about the kids and what they had accomplished.** We learned she was not from Southie, probably Brookline or Newton. But where ever she was from she was the "real deal". **Nothing was about her, it was all about the kids and the other people who contributed their time and their talents.** Everyone from the janitor of one of the public buildings to a professional, very good, artist from Southie. It started to become clear as to how much time and energy had gone into this program. As we gathered closer on the sidewalk to hear the speakers who were scheduled we also saw how simple the event was. There was a portable speaker and microphone, a number of people gathered without much fanfare, a cop the Mayor had probably sent over to help if necessary, and the every day happenings of a busy part of the city. The noise from the street was very challenging for those who spoke.

One very nice introduction was that of a family from Southie whose young daughter and her older sister had painted one of the lighthouses.

They had painted a lighthouse of themselves. When you saw the little girl it was easy to see which lighthouse she had painted. It was really incredible to see how this little girl had captured herself in the painting. From when I first saw her, she bounced about as a lot of little girls do. Something like our nieces Sara and Elizabeth. When you saw the painting of the little girl with blond pony tails, you could see the bouncing in the way she had painted the hair, and especially the pony tails. As the family was introduced there was no doubt who was who. The older sister, who looked older in the painting and the little brother whose painting made him look like the pain in the ass he probably is in real life. Although it was not the BEST PAINTING in the lot it certainly had the best character from my point of view, and most importantly it was HAPPY. ***A happy story about a family from Southie. No alcohol, no yelling or harsh words, and no self made despair.*** The family, in real life was exactly like the painting, just like we would like a lower middle class family in the US to be. Except for their white skin, blond hair, although the young boy had dark hair, there was no way to tell if they were Irish, or something else. ***I of course saw them as Irish, but that's because I see a lot of things through my memory and upbringing. I am not as good as I would like to be at recognizing change.***

As we listened to the speakers and Erin explain who each speaker was and what their lot was in life, something really sad happened. A young man and woman, about mid twenties, walked into the area of the sidewalk where the ceremony was taking place. They were way overweight, looked really slow and made their way through the area by going out into the street, looking dumbfounded as they passed. To me, they were the Irish I knew a long time ago in Southie, probably on the dole, not educated and with not much of a future. Was it my memory and upbringing, or was it the dumb look on their face and the plastic bags full of snack food and soda that they both were carrying. *It was like watching an old dilapidated wooden row boat floating in a fog through a small sea of brightly colored, shinny new sail boats that were sailing along on a sunny summer day.*

It really doesn't matter what it was that burned that incident into my mind, the fact is, *it was sad and reminded me of what we cannot do in this country. We cannot leave anyone behind.* It also made me think of all the hard work it had taken to pull this whole lighthouse painting thing off. *Seeing both of these incidents, the lighthouse happening and the sad Irish couple made me think that even with all the change taking place through the efforts of so many to encourage diversity and the economic growth of South Boston over the past twenty years, the past is still right at hand. "Never ask for whom the bell tolls, the bell tolls for thee"* and, of course, *"there but for the grace of God goes me".*

There are changes taking place in Southie, and in many other neighborhood throughout Boston and far beyond. We as Americans are much better off economically, and hopefully as people of the world. Remember, *"each immigrant makes America more American",* but does more American mean better? I don't know. Certainly the lighthouse project demonstrated the great diversity that exists in Southie now, but does it make it better, or *will we leave the old dilapidated wooden rowboat to float around in the fog?* A very important part of being American to me is always remembering where I came from and how important it is to always *give something back.* Again, the lighthouse project certainly demonstrated, way beyond what I have ever done, how people give something back. *All the people at the ceremony who spoke certainly have done their share in giving something back, and*

I think the results will certainly show in the lives of the kids who participated. I hope these kids will remember what was done for them and remember to give something back when it is their turn.

A sad footnote to this story is that some of the lighthouse paintings were stolen, but then, after the Boston Herald carried a front page story about the actions of the cowards, they were returned thanks to an anonymous tip to the police. ***It's as I said, our past is still right at hand, but I hope "more American" means a better America. I hope I always have ten percent of the energy the people who ran the Lighthouse Project have, they certainly made a part of America better. Thank you.***

<u>*Pride and Imagination*</u>

(I wrote this poetry when President Obama was elected during his inauguration parade. It drives home the meaning of the talent or strength called Significance that I have discussed as one of my talents. Hopefully it will help the reader discover things that he/she considers are significant in their own life. Following the poetry is a short story to explain in more detail how I got to meet JFK and hold on to that 'significant' moment throughout my life)

How many times I told people how I saw JFK when I was a kid
Proud moments for a poor kid from small town
An Irish link that was so much more in imagination than real life
We must be something alike and now he was the president
Eyes left to the reviewing stand for all the marchers in the parade
Bright smiles coming back to each and every kid
Proud moments for poor kids from all over
A Black link that was so much more in imagination than real life
Now there was something very much alike as he is the president
Change, change, change, or is it the same
Proud moments are for all kids now
How happy we should be for the Black kids, it's their turn to dream
How many times they will tell how they saw President Obama
How happy we should be for all kids now that he is president
Finally, a small, bright smiling, Black kid will be just a "happy kid"

Meeting JFK and seeing President Obama

As a teenager, I got to spend summers at a really nice place on Cape Cod. My mother was the housekeeper of a reasonably expensive guest house on the beach in Yarmouth MA. We would spend most of the summer at this place and I got to meet and know some kids from a completely different economic class than what I was accustomed to in my home town. I also got to do some odd jobs to earn myself a pretty good allowance to keep up with my new friends. My mother was best friends with the woman who owned the guest house. She also owned the nursing home my mother worked at in the winter that was next to my house. During the summer of 1959 when I was 14 or 15 the owner of the guest house allowed a friend of mine's brother to use her beach as a place to teach people how to water ski. We, of course, got to do a lot of water skiing for free and would always help out during the lessons. That summer, Mrs. Kennedy was one of the students learning to water ski and on occasion I got to show her how to do different things, like skiing with only one ski and starting in a standing position. Although I knew she was important, and her husband was a senator, I did not think much of it, being only 14. On two or three days during her lessons, JFK brought her to her lesson and waited the half hour or so while she skied. He was always very nice and thanked us for helping to show her how to do different things on the skis. After he announced he would run for President, the water skiing lessons had to be moved to the Kennedy Compound for security reasons. We never got to go there with my friends brother the instructor, but one evening when JFK returned to Cape Cod we, and a bunch of other kids, went up to Hyannis to see him address a crowd of people in the center. It was late August, so the crowd was kind of small and we got to get up pretty close to where he was speaking. As he moved to the podium *my friend and I caught his eye and he gave us a big wave and hello.* It still didn't mean all that much to me, but when he became President, it started to sink in, I had met the President, quite a feat for a kid named Butchie. When ever I told this story, I felt significant and believe this is one of the reasons *significance* is one of my strongest strengths or *talents.*

When I saw the inauguration of President Obama and the kids marching in the parade, I noticed how they would try to catch the eye of the President as they marched past his reviewing stand. The announcer on the TV mentioned that they had been told not to alter their marching to see the President, so the majority of the kids would strain to get their eyes to the left in hopes of catching the eye of the President without altering their marching. I could not help to see the similarities of what they did with President Obama and what I did with JFK. I have always hoped those kids got the same feeling of ***significance*** from seeing the President as I did in seeing JFK. Being recognized by someone special goes a long way with a young kid, even when that kid turns into an adult.

The first Chatham A's game of the 2006 season

(This story was written in 2006 and in an odd way shows how deep emotional talents can be in a person and how they can effect a persons thought process and how they think of themselves. This story kind of goes all over the place, so read it a couple of times and you will get to know what emotional talents sound like to me.)

This is the first time I have gone to Cape Cod and, without planning in advance, showed up in Chatham on the day of the home opener for the A's. Before we left Boston I got a copy of the Chatham A's schedule and there it was: Chatham A's home opener against Harwich at Veterans Field on June 15 @ 7pm. Sweeeet!!! I get to watch the opener of the best college baseball in the country at my favorite place on the Cape. I can never really figure out why I love it here so much. Maybe it is the memories of when I was a kid, and at 5 or 6 years old my mother would find a way to get us to the Cape for a week in July, or when I got a bit older and my mother worked for Mrs. Maloney at the guest house in Yarmouth. The times when I was 5 or 6 we would go to Dennisport and rent a cottage from Mr. Eddy who owned Eddy's Silver Camps. They were these really small cottages built on the sand very close to the water. They consisted of one big room that served as kitchen, living room, bedroom, and a private bedroom and a bathroom with a stall shower. Our days were entirely at the beach with a visit to the Chowder Bowl, if you were lucky, for a piece of a frozen Charleston Chew. Mr. Eddy could break a Charleston Chew into the smallest pieces so everyone would get a piece. If the weather was bad you got to learn how sand fleas lived, as you would be relegated to the cottage with eight or ten other people with nothing to do.

When I graduated to Yarmouth, it was quite different. The Guest House my mother worked at called the Ocean Terrace Lodge was at Englewood Beach and directly on the water. It was in an upscale neighborhood and yours truly, Butchie Cleggett was certainly out of his element. I would do odd jobs at the guesthouse and make a good allowance so I could mix, "appropriately" with the neighborhood kids. *It gave me my champagne appetite on my father's less than beer income.* My father worked as a Burner/Welder at the Fore River Ship Yard in Quincy, MA. You won't hear a lot about him in these stories; I really do not like the memories of him and what he meant to me. All in all though my life has worked out okay, but that's a story for a different time. This is a tale of the first Chatham A's game of the 2006 season.

Kathy and I arrived at the Bradford Inn at about 3pm and immediately took one of our favorite walks around the loop. Its about 3 miles and goes to the Chatham light and through the center of town. We finished in about and hour and came back to the Bradford. We are staying in the main inn so I opened a bottle of my $4.50 George deBoeuf Chardonnay, and we had drinks on the second floor porch while the sun set. Kathy had her usual whiskey and ginger ale (hold the whiskey) and I was very content in getting back to Jim Cleggett's style of drinking what tasted good as long as it was cheap. We also had some good Irish cheese and our usual crackers. We sat for about an hour and decided to go to the game early and have dinner later.

We left the hotel and walked to Veteran's Field. As we passed the Mobil station we noticed the school at the field was being renovated and there was a fence around it that kept you from going to the field. I also noticed the usual sign saying there was a game was not at the rt.28 rotary. We continued up rt. 28 to another entrance to the field and made it to the third base side of the field. The field looked good, very green and lush, but the infield looked in disarray. It was then that we realized that there were no players and very few fans. Although it looked like a great night for a ball game we were soon told that the game had been cancelled due to the field conditions. Apparently the rain earlier in the day had made the field unplayable, and the word of mouth announcing system had not reached the Cleggett's at the Bradford.

Okay, so why a tale about the first Chatham A's game, it had been cancelled you dope. Well that's why there is a story, because what we did instead of seeing the game is something we wouldn't have done if there was a game, and ***I like telling stories about good things that happen to me by chance.*** Like the story about the two kids flying to Florida who were sitting beside me in the last row of the plane when I, as Joseph D. Cleggett, Sr. Vice President of the very prestigious Jacobs Engineering Company, always gets a seat up front on an aisle. As I entered the plane, having changed my reservation two or three times, I realized "up front on an aisle" had become row 27. In a 737, there are 28 rows of seats, and you can be sure the numbering goes from 1 to 28 and not the reverse. After accepting that I was going to row 27, I thought, "Oh well, it could be worse", as I saw there were no screaming kids in the vicinity of row 27. As I turned into the row, there they were, two, not one, seven or eight year old twin boys. The stewardess was quick to point out that they were in her charge and we were all going to have a great time. ***Oh yeah, you can bet on that, two snot nosed kids and one irritable Harp for a 3 hour hop to Ft. Lauderdale.*** It turned out to be one of the best experiences of my life that I will tell you about later, or, if I ever do publish all this nonsense, you will be able to read about. (The rest of the story is coming up next in the story entitled Two Kids on a Plane)

For now it's the baseball story. Kathy and I sat on the third base line, knowing there was no game, but it wasn't until the announcer, who actually came to the game, told us (three times) that there would be no game that we decided to leave and go have dinner. Our dinner was somewhat uneventful. We went to Christian's at the East end of Chatham center. We ate upstairs at the bar where we always eat. John Frazier, our friend and the head bartender was not there and Bobby, who is a nice guy, was in his *usual friendly, suck up mode to the other "rich regulars" at the bar.* The conversation was as always, "we're rich", "we're richer" and of course, "we're the rich, richer". "Our kids go to this BEST school" and "our kids go to this BEST, BEST school". "We came a day early this week so we can take the boat to the Vineyard for a few days, so we are the richest and went to the BEST OF ALL School. These summertime Cape Coders from Brookline, Belmont, New York, New Jersey and where ever didn't know *they had Jim Cleggett's son Butchie sitting with them who went to the BEST, BEST, BEST, Braintree High School, Wentworth Institute and Northeastern University nights, and made as much in an hour as Jim made in a week.* That makes me better and richer, RIGHT? WHY, WHY, WHY do I like it here? *How can I sit at this bar and smile at these people and tell myself they are really okay and I am just like them?* I hope this story will help you find out the answers to these questions. After some more BLAH, BLAH, BLAH, some short glasses of wine and Kathy's whiskey and ginger ale (hold the whiskey) we left and decided to walk to the water near the Chatham Bars Inn.

You should realize that we have been coming to Chatham for about 20 years. For about 15 or those years we stayed at the Chatham Bars Inn until it just *became too expensive and too pretentious.* It is a really great spot, but enough is enough----too much money. We moved to the Bradford Inn that is much more the Butchie Cleggett type of place. Each year though we make it a point to go back to the Inn and have a drink on the porch or to check in on Ray, a really nice bartender who has lived in Chatham all his life. ***It is like checking in on a place where we made some great memories with a real person like Ray.*** Ray was in the Navy for 20 years and has a government pension. He is a very consistent person, never sucking up to anyone, and always ***knowing his place***. What a terrible thing to say, "Knowing his place", but that is how he is. As long as I have known him and as friendly as I have tried to be, I am still a customer to Ray.

[Just a short note about people "knowing their place" and other sayings that really get my goat: one in particular. I have a 'friend' I worked with for about seven years. He is the great grandson of one of the founders of the Company and reasonably wealthy. He comes from "old money" as those in the know would say. One day he was talking about another friend's wife and made the comment "she is not cut from the same cloth". I didn't think much about it until a month or so later when we were talking about his mother. His father had married his nurse, having been stricken with polio at a young age. She had been complaining about having to go to New Hampshire to one of their houses where there were not sufficient hired hands to do all the work. I tried a weak defense for the woman, commenting on what she had given up marrying a person with polio, even though he was one of the haves. My friend got really pissed and said; "she has had everything since she married my father, an upstairs maid, a downstairs maid, a driver, etc, etc, etc. And again I said, "But it must have been hard, especially when they were young with you and your brothers." He turned to me, and with a hateful look, said; "you don't understand, she is not cut from the same cloth". What a terrible thing to say about your mother, or about anyone for that matter. I had to tell that story, so I never

forget about all the cloth my mother and father pieced together to come up with the burlap sack they made me from. For a very long part of my life I thought all people with money were the BEST. Not so, people are what they are no matter what they have.]

It was a really nice night, the way spring should be on Cape Cod. We left the water and as always walked through the Inn's property and then decided to go to the bar to see if Ray was working. Sure enough, there he was, all 130 pounds of him smiling and doing his thing. I walked up and shook hands and asked him how he was since his by pass operation. He said "fine" and his look told me that he really appreciated one of his customers actually taking the time to ask how he was doing. More than that*: it was that someone in the Chatham Bars Inn on the other side of the bar actually cared about Ray.*

Anyway this is the story I have been trying to tell you. Kathy and I sat and talked with Ray for about an hour. I had a couple of cups of coffee, and Kathy had her usual, the whiskey with ginger ale (hold the whiskey). We talked about our operations, where we had them, how long we stayed in the hospital, how they found the problem and how we were doing physically. I had mine 4 years ago; Ray had his about 2.5 years ago. *There were times during this conversation when Ray and I were on the same side of the bar.* Earlier, at Christian's I didn't fit on either side of the bar. I am lucky, have done really well, for someone named Butchie, *and always tried to be on the right side of the bar, and appreciate people on both sides.* I really feel good when I can put it all aside and talk to someone like Ray. When we went to leave I wanted to give Ray a great tip for all he had done for us over the years and asked him for the bill. He looked at me with that great smile and said very honestly *"this one is on me".* What a great *feeling* came over me. *I met another real person whom I will*

care about forever. Ray probably would read this story and think ***"what a bunch of BS"*** and that would be okay. I will keep this memory forever and ***remember how important it is to know, and more importantly respect, people on both sides of the bar.*** Well, that's the story of the Chatham A's first game of the 2006 season, and quite a game it was:

Chatham 0, Harwich 0, Butchie Cleggett 100.

Two Kids on a Plane

(This story was written in 2002 and is used here to help explain why it is so important to stay positive about yourself and others. It is also a story I never want to forget, and I always said I would publish it some day, so here it is. You should be able to get some lessons out of it on ways to stay positive when life is not going your way. Try talking to yourself the same way I talk to myself and see if it doesn't help with controlling your ego and consciousness when dealing with others.)

This is a very short story that I always want to remember. As we grow in business we take on more responsibility and tend to worry about 'whatever'. We also tend to forget about what is going on around us and the people we meet on a daily basis. We can easily not see the full value of people we meet because we are too wrapped up in our own concerns of business and BS. During my career I have spent a considerable amount of time traveling, mostly by air, with at least one trip a week. After a while it gets old and I lost my ability to really enjoy people. It seemed there was always some problem with the airport, the flight, my seat, or something. After 911 traveling got even worse. One positive thing I did during this time was to read more. Reading helped me to calm down and the books I read on management and leadership helped me to realize the importance of people. I think the events of September 11th also helped me to focus more on what was going on around me, especially the people, while traveling. (I became much more conscious of my surroundings) It helped me realize 'we are all in the same boat, so lets at least be kind to each other'.

I decided to try something in an effort to take my mind off the 'battle' of travel. I would work at making someone feel better by helping him or her, giving them a kind word, or just listening. As I began this 'new attitude' my help usually came while the plane was boarding; helping someone with his or her bags, or just a smile when someone expected me to be annoyed. For a while it was working really well and I began to feel pretty good about myself and about traveling.

Then one day it all seemed to go in the bucket. I was traveling to Florida for a weekly meeting. The weather was really poor and the flight was delayed before we even boarded. Things got worse when I realized the plane was overbooked and loading would also be delayed. When we finally started to board, I realized my 'up front on an aisle' seat was in row 27 of a 28 row aircraft. As I approached this 'up front' seat I noticed my two seat pals were seven year old twin boys. I quickly realized that the only luck I was having today was 'bad' luck. Just before I abandoned my new *(positive)* attitude I thought to myself "oh well, new attitude, practice what you preach, never loose a chance to make someone feel good". I said "Hi Fella's", and the boys responded with a shy "Hi" probably because they had been told 'not to talk to strangers'. I continued by asking "how they were doing" and they replied "OK" again, not too enthusiastically, but by this time I was determined to continue with my new *(positive)* attitude. As we sat on the runway waiting I learned they were two seven year old boys who had been visiting Grandma and Grandpa in New Hampshire for two weeks and were now on their way home to Orlando where their divorced mother and father lived.

Their mother was a juvenile probations officer and their father was studying to be a physical education teacher at Florida State University. After waiting about twenty minutes, we were ready to take off and the flight attendant was giving the (safety) instructions. During the instructions when the attendant says "in case of an emergency" one boy asks about the oxygen mask, "What's that for"? I respond, "Well if there's a problem, you put it on". He looks at me with a lot of concern on his face and says "What kind of a problem"? I respond and say "Don't worry it's just for safety" and of course he says "Why"? and I say "Well, if the air in the plane

..........and I pause, and the other boy jumps in and says "Oh if it stinks'? And I say "Yea, that's it, if the air smells, we put on the mask" (sounds reasonable, they're only seven) and before I can say anything else, the other boy says "So if I fart we have to put on the mask" and we all laugh. The boys really laugh and I realize the concern is over. The rest of the flight was great. I learned about Tyler and Bret Montogomery and their one year old brother Zachary.

As I left the plane I stopped to tell their father that he had two great kids. As I walked away the father asked "Who is he"? One of the boys replied "He's the man who helped us on the plane".

I learned a really good lesson. Never pass up the chance to make someone, (even, or maybe 'especially' two seven year old boys) feel good. ***That day I became a better person***. Thanks kids.

The Flight Attendant

(This is a story I thought of after reading Two Kids on a Plane. It happened about a month after my very positive experience with those two twin boys. I have to think my revitalized positive thinking came about after my experience with the Two Kids on a Plane. I wanted to include this story, because it is a great example of one of my favorite sayings that you will read about a lot in this book: 'Always do the right thing, it doesn't have to happen'. This story about The Flight Attendant is a perfect example of 'doing the right thing' and going a little further so 'it' doesn't happen.)

I was traveling on one of my routine, probably weekly, trips from Tampa to Boston just about a month after my trip to Orlando with The Two Kids on a Plane. The trip had gone well and although Tampa is not one of my favorite airports, all was going well, the plane was on time, not overcrowded, and I was back to my 'up front on an aisle' status, and may have even been upgraded to first class. The plane left on time, good take off, and we were up in the 'wild blue yonder' headed for Boston when the pilot announced we had to go back as there was a problem with some instrument on the plane. As he started his turn over the Gulf of Mexico to head back to Tampa, I noticed he appeared to be turning the plane with the wing and the turn was really wide and slow. Although I am not a pilot or airplane expert, all of my flying has given me some experience and I got the impression there was something more than an instrument problem. As we approached Tampa it was clear that there was some sort of emergency as the tarmac had been cleared of all other planes.

Just so you know I am not crazy, an older woman sitting across the aisle from me apparently shared my concern, as she asked if "I would hold her hand during the landing". I did of course, and the landing although

171

a bit bumpy went fine. The pilot came on and told us the problem had to do with instruments that control the tail section of the aircraft and that we would have to change planes, and that there would be a new crew. In an effort to speed things up and get us on our way, we would all take the same seat on the new plane and be shuttled to the new gate.

All went really well and in about an hour we were on the new plane and getting ready to go. I had struck up a conversation with a lawyer who was sitting next to me about exercising some stock options I had and was engrossed in the conversation when the new flight attendant started to give the safety instructions. Now you have to understand something, I was on the Corporate Safety Committee of a very large International Engineering Corporation who's 'primary' concern is the safety of their employees, and I take safety very seriously. My work discipline to this day is Safety, Quality, Financials, and People.

As the attendant started her instructions, I asked the lawyer to be quiet so I could give the attendant my attention. As I sat back in my seat, the attendant looked at me and said, "That's it, you're off this flight, you're not paying attention to my instructions". The lawyer intervened, as did the person sitting next to me, but the attendant remained adamant, "No you're off" as she started towards the door to the flight deck (the plane was actually rolling away from the gate). I stood up, opened the overhead compartment to get my bag when the other flight attendant from the back of the plane came running up the aisle and told me to sit down. I looked at him and said "She just told me I had to leave". By this time she had notified the pilot and the plane had stopped and the pilot was coming out of the cockpit. The pilot intervened and asked what the problem was. The flight attendant gave her version of what had happened and I gave mine. As the pilot listened to each account a very elderly gentleman who was sitting in the first row spoke up and said "She (referring to the flight attendant) has got a real problem, he didn't do anything". The pilot took her aside and the problem was resolved with me staying on the flight.

Now for the heart of the story. After we took off and were back in the 'wild blue yonder' the flight attendant has to serve me a drink and some snacks. She approaches me in a sheepish way and says "What would you like"? And I say "I would like you to sit down here, (in the aisle seat across from mine) and resolve this" Much to my surprise, she does and I explain why I was talking when she started her instructions. She then tells me that she was not scheduled for the flight and it really was an inconvenience as she was headed home for the weekend. She goes on to say that there was some kind of emergency and a flight had to return to the airport and she had to work. I tell her that we were the emergency and it was kind of a lousy situation for everyone. She did not know she was on the plane that replaced the plane that had the emergency. We both paused for a minute and then she looked at me with tears in her eyes and said "I'm really sorry, I was in a really bad mood and took it out on you". I said, "Yea, but at least we worked it out, you were willing to sit down and talk about it, and that makes it fine with me". We actually hugged and that was the end of it.

The moral of this story is simple; *'do the right thing, it doesn't have to happen'*. I could have just had her get me a drink when she asked "What would you like", but I didn't, because I knew how important it was to make sure this situation did not go any further. I used to fly a lot and I knew she, and the pilot, would have to write a report about this incident and I did not want her to write a report that would put me on any special negative list with the airline. After we landed I waited for the pilot and told him I was sorry for the problem. He told me that all was okay and thanked me for talking to the flight attendant. *If you are consciously working to be positive and have your ego in your shoe* all you have to do is take *'doing the right thing'* a little further and you can ensure that *'it' will not happen*.

The Ninth Grade Dance

(This is a story about a dance I had with a really nice girl when I was in the Ninth grade, about fourteen years old. I was lucky to be popular in school and even luckier to meet someone, by chance, not as popular as me who would have a positive effect on my life forever. This story goes along with my Azel Road story where I believe my emotional talents took root. At six years old, I was aware of my feelings for others the day I wanted to go to the park and my mother was sad being left alone at home. I knew the exact spot on Azel Road where my feelings overwhelmed me and started my four lane highways on emotional talents, understanding the feelings of others. Eight years later, at fourteen, the four lane highway was just about complete and my talents on caring for the feelings of others were well founded. I believe this shows that talents are founded at a young age and grow until you are a teenager, developing your character. Read the story and see what you think.)

This story takes place in May or June of 1959 at the Junior High School I attended. At that time, our school system was broken down into three sections, K-6, 7-9, and 10-12. Being a ninth grader was like being a senior in Jr. High School. The ninth grade dance was like the Senior Prom of the Jr. High School, no seventh or eighth graders were allowed to attend, it was all for the BIG kids. We all arrived at the dance, held in the gymnasium of the school, at about seven pm and went to our *'popular kids corner'* to be admired by all. I am sure you know that in the ninth grade, the boys are on one side and the girls are on the other, and never the twain shall meet. As the evening progressed, the teacher chaperones were encouraging all to dance, much to no avail. At about eight pm, the principal of the school, a really nice man came over to our *'popular kids corner'* and told us that we should be sure that "no girl went home without a dance". Then he turned to me, as he was a friend of my family, and said "make sure that (this particular girl) had a dance". (I cannot state the name because I was not able to contact her for this story, but believe me I have never forgotten her name, or her great smile.) So, I did as told and asked her to dance. After the first dance, I asked for another and after that, I got her some punch. At the beginning of the first dance, I believed I was doing her a favor at the request of the principal, as she was not one of the popular kids in school. I had done what the principal asked and felt pretty good about myself, thinking I made this non-popular girl feel good. I went on back to the *'popular kids corner'* with my friends and she went back to her friends. The dance continued and we did not see each other again that night. Some of my friends gave me a hard time for dancing 'two' dances with her and then getting her punch, saying all I really had to do was the one dance. I brushed it off and told them to forget it as I only did what the principal asked as he was a friend of my mother. I took some ribbing from my friends for a while but just like everything else that happens when you are fourteen; it is soon forgotten by all.

What wasn't forgotten is that by the end of the night, I had made a new friend and believed I was the lucky one. I had seen this girl almost every day from the seventh grade to the ninth grade and never noticed her as she was kind of heavy and not popular. After that night and those two dances, I only saw her once or twice again that year, but each time she would give me that great smile and a warm 'hello'. This greeting by her continued all throughout high school and I had truly made a new friend the night of the **Ninth Grade Dance**. I have often wondered who the principal was trying to help, the unpopular girl or the *'star struck'* fourteen year old.

When you finish High School and get your Year Book, it is common to have your friends sign the book under their picture. When I asked this girl to sign my book, she wrote "Remember the ninth grade dance". Although I am sure she will *'probably'* never read this story, Ann can be sure that I have never forgotten the **Ninth Grade Dance**, and I am sure she *'probably'* still has a great smile. I have danced with a lot of people throughout life and with the exception of those dances with my wife, not many have been as memorable as the dances I had with Ann in the Ninth Grade. I am very lucky to have well formed emotional talents that started early in life and grew into strengths that have helped me succeed with people throughout my career and life. I owe a lot to my mother for giving me those talents that she had and always used as a nurse caring for others. I also owe a lot to the many people throughout my life that have cared enough about me to give me time and advice, showing me they cared for others well being. Luckily, empathy and the emotionally sensitive talents can be learned by highlighting your self awareness and forcing yourself to be aware of others feelings and values, and it is well worth the effort.

<u>*Five Women and a Really Big Little Boy*</u>

The story I am going to tell you is about five women and one little boy who are probably the main reason I was able to write this book. When I first thought of this story, it was going to be the dedication of the book, but as it developed it was clear that there was a lot of good examples of where **talents** and **disciplines** come from and the importance of being brought up in a ***free society***. I hope you will learn from my experiences where your talents and disciplines come from by examining relationships in your life through your own short stories. Women, usually mothers, have a tremendous influence on the lives of children and as we know talents and disciplines are developed at a really young age and subject to this influence. Look back at your early life and see if there weren't some people who had an influence on you and helped develop your talents, strengths and disciplines.

"Little Women"

There was a book when I was a kid with the title **"Little Women"**. It was about four women and their friends who lived during the Civil War. The book was just about required reading for girls in the primary grades of school. So what has this got to do with you learning what your talents are? Probably nothing, but it does have something to say about one of the key *'ingrained prejudices'* that I have tried to bring attention to throughout the book and that I will continue to work on with this short story about five women in my life and a really big little boy. Some believed the title of this book **'Little Women'** was intended to highlight the inferiority of women as compared to men. The Civil War took place in 1863 or so and even then someone found it necessary to write about women, and the important role they have played in the history of this country and the world. So why are there ten times as many men in leadership positions as women, especially now after another hundred and fifty years or so? How long are we going to put up with this *'ingrained prejudice'* in our evaluation of women? I could also make a point for how children impact our lives, but that will come out in the story.

The first of these five women in my life was my mother, **Eva Mae Tyson**. She was born in Prince Edward Island Canada while her mother, father and older brother were on their way from Blackpool England to the United States as immigrants. As my mother grew up in the US, her father owned a bar and grill type restaurant called "Tom's Grill" and did well in the business. My mother went to a private girls school and after that married my father and began her life of raising five children and putting up with a husband who drank too much and lacked any real compassion towards my mother and her ambitions. Still, my mother became a nurse and worked nights most of her life at a nursing home next to our house to earn money that would mostly be spent on her kids. She also continued being a more than full time mother always available for school events and the such. Being the youngest of the five, by six years, I was always still aware of what my mother did for her kids and how little my father did to support her efforts to see that we all had dancing or music lessons and lived as much of a privileged life as she could give us, wanting us to have what she had as a kid. It was really easy to learn how to care for others by just being around my mother and watching her *empathy talents* and the *emotional strengths* she had in caring for others, always before herself. When I think of how I feel about people and equality, I know where these talents come from; they come from my mother. There is no better way to acquire a *'four lane talent'* than to see it being practiced every day by someone you respect, especially when you are at a really young age. At five years old,

I would go to the nursing home when I got home from school to wait for my father to get home from work and watch my mother help the old people in the home. As I think back, she did it with a lot of love and care, every day and never complained. It was a perfect example of the ***definition of a talent, strength and discipline,*** she did her work ***'repeatedly, happily, and successfully'***, and I got to watch. So, the first woman gave me my ***talent of empathy,*** my ***strength of emotional EQ,*** and my ***discipline of always doing more than what is expected.*** How about you, is there someone in your life that affected you like my mother affected me?

The second of these five women is my mother-in-law, **Mary Magdalene Richard**. She was born in the US and came into my life when I was sixteen, and started dating my wife. Mary was someone who had been brought up in the depression in a family that may have lost something financially, but she never lost her character as a solid human being. She worked as the ***'stay at home mom'*** while her husband Andy worked as a Postal Superintendent. I always believed that Mary wanted to pass on her own life's ambitions to her children. She valued education and always showed its importance to her children and me by demonstrating the strength of reading and studying history. She had an interest in politics that found its way into my ambitions and once again helped to show me the strength of caring for others, similar to what my own mother did. As I look back on what I learned from Mary, I think of a favorite saying I use, ***'plan your work and work your plan'***. This saying is really a discipline that I have developed over my lifetime and I have to think that knowing Mary helped me to understand and respect the full meaning of planning what you want to accomplish, changing your goals and continuing on even if you are defeated. My political career was very important to the development of my leadership skills and Mary was one of my *'four lane highways'* in that area. She was a quality person and helped me to develop and use my *'significance strength'* properly. When you need to be significant, you can really overlook some very important aspects in how you handle success and defeat. Mary helped to keep me grounded in dealing with people and helped me to respect myself in any situation. I think I learned my basic discipline of planning and doing from my technical education and strict upbringing, Mary helped me to tailor it to make it more acceptable to all, even those I did not like. One of my signature strengths is *'consistency'* in that I am *'keenly aware of the need to treat people the same, no matter what their station in life.'* I learned this very important trait from someone who demonstrated it every day I knew her. Mary, much like my mother did this *'repeatedly, happily and successfully'* and I got to watch and improve on my skills and knowledge to develop the really good *signature strength of 'consistency'.*

The third of these five women (and by the way all five women are number one in my book) is my daughter **Erin Amanda Munroe.** Erin is someone who always exceeds my expectations, and makes me really think, as she does things much differently than I do, but usually succeeds. Watching this has made me realize the importance of my signature theme *'individualization' respecting the 'unique qualities of each person'* and getting to hear the *'one-of–a –kind stories of each persons life'.* She, by the way, has authored three books of her own and is presently working on the fourth and can tell really great stories. I like to hear peoples stories, Erin has helped me listen and learn how others think and appreciate them for their talents. It is very interesting to watch someone (especially someone you love) with the same ethnic background tell stories about their life and how things have changed in just one generation. Erin sees some of the same things I saw years ago in a much different way and listening to her in her books and stories has been an education in itself. You can be sure I never would have written this book if it wasn't for Erin. Erin also introduced me to **"The Four Agreements"** a book that suggests four steps in dealing with other people: *'be impeccable to your word, don't take anything personally, don't make assumptions, and always do your best.'* Really good advice for someone writing a book on 'Creating a Leadership Discipline'. These four steps have become the backbone of my *'Communications Strength'*, something I have had for a long time that needed some 'tweaking' as I got older and wiser. I have learned a lot from Erin and watching, knowing and loving her makes me a better person every day. You might want to include some stories of people younger than yourself when you are trying to find out where your talents and strengths come from.

The fourth of these five women kind of needs a special introduction, as she would want it that way, so here goes:

Evelyn Violet Munroe

Evelyn Violet Munroe is my granddaughter. She is three (almost four) years old going on about fifteen. On one occasion when her father was asking her to drink her chocolate milk from a glass and not the container, and she was ignoring him, she finally answered by saying "I am drinking my chocolate milk in Spanish, and you are speaking to me in English, so I do not understand." On another occasion when her six year old brother asked his mother "why he always did what Evelyn wanted", his mother answered "because you let her get away with it". This is a kid that we can all learn from. I have no idea what makes her tick or how she comes up with the things she says, but I do know that she is a bit of a conniver. She loves to ignore her Grandpa to let him know who sets the rules that include; no kisses, no hugs, unless she really needs one, and only 'high fives' on her conditions. You're probably asking 'why is she one of the five women in his life? Well it is simple. My first *Significant Theme or Strength* is called *'Significance'* and it means that a lot of my drive comes from my wanting to be *'significant in the eyes of other people, I want to be heard, to stand out for the unique strengths I possess'*. This may seem like a negative, but believe me it isn't, it has given me the drive and desire to always do my best. So how does *Evelyn* help with my need to recognize my *'Significance Strength'*? When she comes to our house, she will talk to my wife and completely ignore me until she decides that it is time to recognize Grandpa. However, if I listen closely, while she talks with my wife, usually in another room from where I am, I sometimes here her say, in a very nonchalant way *"where's Grandpa"*, and once again, I am *'Significant' to Evelyn*. On a serious note, understanding and recognizing your talents and strengths is very important and you can do that in a number of ways. Sometimes the best way is to think your three year old granddaughter believes you to be *'Significant'*. It is really amazing what you can learn from kids, after all, they are learning from you and you might want to know how they interpret what you do by watching what they believe is important to them.

The next of the five is my grandson who I better give the same special introduction as I gave his sister, "or else" as he would say.

Gavin Andrew Munroe

Gavin Andrew Munroe is my grandson. He is six years old and the youngest kid in his first grade class and also the biggest. The expression *'little big man'* really fits describing his age and size, but certainly not his personality. He is a great kid, always telling stories with a great imagination and desire to be heard. He also talks quite a bit like his Grandpa whom if you remember was *'most talkative'* in his high school class. If ever I have to see my talents of *imagination, communication, or significance* and how they developed, all I have to do is spend some time with *Gavin,* and there they are, being developed once again by a six year old. *Gavin* is also developing tremendous *emotional talents* at this young age that show in how *sensitive and protective* he is of his younger sister. He and I go to breakfast sometimes at a local restaurant that always has a lollypop for him when he finishes. He never leaves without one for *Evelyn* as well as the one for himself, and he did this on his own, without any coaching. No matter where we go and what we do he always includes something for her in a really nice way. As a six year old he also competes for attention with her and there are some instances where his ego gets a bit damaged and he has to take a time out. Watching him mature over the last two years, has really been exciting. You can see the changes in how he responds to challenging events, and you can see that they are going to be really good friends no matter how competitive the situation. He is really learning to *put his ego in his shoe* when dealing with *Evelyn*. The best part about *Gavin* is his *stories and his imagination*. He will tell me some concoction of an event, like his teacher coming back from a vacation and her plane landing in the school parking lot and when he sees that I know it is probably not the case, he will look at me, laugh and say, *"I was only fooling Grandpa"*. It isn't so much the story but the use of his *imagination and communication skills* with all the physical emotion he displays that reminds me of myself as a kid. Again, when I want to get some kind of an idea of how *talents* are born at a young age all I have to do is spend time with *Gavin and Evelyn*. At these young ages, the talents are raw and without all the protections we incorporate, that hide our true feelings, as we get older. If you want to see how talents are born and developed, find kids like Gavin and Evelyn in your life and watch them as they develop for a few years, you'll learn more than even you can *imagine.* I know I did, and I like to think my best talent is my *imagination.*

The last of the five women in my life is my wife, *Kathy Hoagland*. I like to call her that because I love to remember how much of a person she was before I even met her. All of what you have or will read in this book and most of what happened to me in my life, in some way, had her signature on it. I met her when I was sixteen, dated her for about seven years, and have been married to her for forty seven years. We, of course, have had our *'trials and tribulations'*, but in the end have survived as a couple, and quite a happy one at that. She is the Executive Editor (a title she dislikes) of this book and most everything I write, including the technical reports for law firms we prepare at Tyson-Richard Consulting. She is also a co-owner of Tyson Richard, and I am sure that by now you have figured out that the company is named after my mother and Kathy's mother. Throughout our time together *Kathy* has had her own successful career in the financial world while bringing up Erin and putting up with me. Her contributions to the development of my talents and strengths have always been given *repeatedly, happily and successfully.* She has never quit on me and always been there through thick and thin. In business and in life, whenever I had to put my *best foot forward, or make a good first impression*, I would bring *Kathy* with me, and it always worked. Most of the executives I worked with knew when I would come up with a good idea using my imagination, or a good business position, that *Kathy* was, in some way, involved. I remember once, when developing a negotiating strategy for a major project and presenting the idea of projecting the strategy forward to a second project, which was seen as a very good idea, the CEO of the company very quickly said, *"I see Ms Cleggett has been involved in*

developing this." In fairness the CEO did know ***Kathy*** as he lived in the same town and had good knowledge of my family and political involvement, but never the less, he knew of her knowledge talents and skills, and how we worked as partners. And that is what a lot of this is about. As you go through this book and work to understand and promote your ***talents,*** look to those who know you the best, your wife, husband or partner and be sure to acknowledge where and how your ***skills have been improved***. You will find it is those intimately around you that have helped make you what you are. In my case, ***Kathy*** is quite different then me in many ways; I talk a lot, she is quiet, I am conservative, she is liberal, I have learned through experience, she is very book smart, I tend to be crude, she is polished, I expect people to live up to my expectations, ***Kathy*** accepts people as they are, and so on and so on .... The point here is that understanding someone very close to you and learning to respect how they see and do things differently can be a tremendous asset to you in learning what your ***talents*** are and how to understand your limits. In all of the differences I mentioned above, I have learned from ***Kathy*** to temper my own thoughts with some of how she sees situations, and the result of my actions has been better for it. I could write another book about how ***Kathy*** has influenced me throughout my life but the real lesson in introducing ***Kathy*** to you is for you to find someone like her that means a lot to you and to honestly learn from that person so that you will honestly understand your ***talents skills and disciplines.***

Five Women and a Really Big Little Boy is a story that I enjoyed writing. It made me remember how important other people are in all phases of life. It also helped me to reinforce my belief that talents start to be developed at a really young age and are usually influenced by people around you in life. The best way for a talent to be developed is to see someone else doing it and wanting to get the same satisfaction they got repeatedly. I am sure my *emotional talents* come from watching my mother, *Eva Mae Tyson*, care for others as a nurse. I would also bet that my disciplines to *'do the right thing so it doesn't have to happen' and 'plan your work and work your plan'* were nurtured by my mother-in-law, *Mary Magdalene Richard.* Understanding people and honestly accepting them for their abilities is the result of watching my daughter, *Erin Munroe*, accomplish what she has in her own way. Reinforcing my belief in my *significance talent and strength* is always provided by the simple little phrase *"where's Grandpa"* spoken by *Evelyn Violet Munroe* and my *communication talents and imagination talent* is evident to me each day I spend with my grandson *Gavin Andrew Munroe.* Last, but certainly not least, all of what I believe in is evident every day just by being with my wife *Kathy Hoagland.* I am very lucky to have all these people around me and I bet you have the same kinds of people around you that can help you learn more about your *talents, skills, strengths and disciplines.*

Endnotes

Prologue

1. Fareed Zakaria, *The Post American World* (New York: W.W. Norton and Company, 2008), 1.
2. Zakaria, *The Post American World*, 190
3. Zakaria, *The Post American World*, 193-194
4. Robert K. Cooper Ph.D. and Ayman Sawaf, *Executive EQ* (New York: Grosset/Putnam, 1997), xiii

Chapter 1 Shortcut

1. Fred Kofman, *Conscious Business* (Boulder, Colorado: Sounds True, 2013) 3
2. Geoff Colvin, *"Humans are Underrated,"* Fortune.com, July 23,2015, 5
3. Colvin, *"Humans are Underrated,"* 5
4. Cooper and Sawaf, *Executive EQ,* xxiv
5. Cooper and Sawaf, *Executive EQ,* xiii
6. Walt Disney (from TV?)

Chapter 2 The Changing World

1. Zakaria, *The Post American World*, 20
2. Geoffrey Brewer and Barb Sanford, eds., Decade of Change (New York: Gallup Press, 2011) 13
3. Brewer and Sanford, *Decade of Change*, 14
4. Brewer and Sanford, *Decade of Change*, 200
5. Marcus Buckingham and Donald O. Clifton, *Now, Discover Your Strengths* (New York: The Free Press, 2001) 98
6. Colvin, *"Humans are Underrated"* 5
7. Colvin, *"Humans are Underrated"* 5
8. Colvin, *"Humans are Underrated"* 5
9. Colvin, *"Humans are Underrated"* 7
10. Colvin, *"Humans are Underrated"* 7
11. Colvin, *"Humans are Underrated"* 8

Chapter 3 Understanding Who You Are

1. Buckingham and Clifton, *Now Discover Your Strengths*, 128
2. Buckingham and Clifton, *Now Discover Your Strengths*, 48
3. Buckingham and Clifton, *Now Discover Your Strengths*, 26
4. Buckingham and Clifton, *Now Discover Your Strengths*, 128
5. Cooper and Sawaf, *Executive EQ*, xiii
6. Buckingham and Clifton, *Now Discover Your Strengths*, 42
7. Buckingham and Clifton, *Now Discover Your Strengths*, 45
8. Buckingham and Clifton, *Now Discover Your Strengths*, 45
9. Buckingham and Clifton, *Now Discover Your Strengths*, 47
10. Cooper and Sawaf, *Executive EQ*, xiii
11. Cooper and Sawaf, *Executive EQ*, xiii
12. Cooper and Sawaf, *Executive EQ*, xiii
13. Cooper and Sawaf, *Executive EQ*, xiii

14. Cooper and Sawaf, *Executive EQ*, xi
15. Cooper and Sawaf, *Executive EQ*, 255
16. Cooper and Sawaf, *Executive EQ*, 256

Chapter 4 Talents

1. Buckingham and Clifton, *Now Discover Your Strengths*, 30
2. Buckingham and Clifton, *Now Discover Your Strengths*, 48
3. Marcus Buckingham andCurt Coffman, *First, Break All the Rules* (New York: Simon and Schuster, 1999) 80
4. Buckingham and Coffman, *First, Break All the Rules*, 81
5. Buckingham and Coffman, *First, Break All the Rules*, 82
6. Buckingham and Clifton, *Now, Discover Your Strengths*, 7
7. Buckingham and Coffman, *First, Break All the Rules*, 82
8. Buckingham and Coffman, *First, Break All the Rules*, 85
9. Buckingham and Clifton, *Now, Discover Your Strengths*, 30
10. Buckingham and Clifton, *Now, Discover Your Strengths*, 29
11. Buckingham and Clifton, *Now, Discover Your Strengths*, 67
12. Buckingham and Coffman, *First, Break All the Rules*, 251
13. Buckingham and Coffman, *First, Break All the Rules*, 251
14. Buckingham and Coffman, *First, Break All the Rules*, 251
15. Buckingham and Coffman, *First, Break All the Rules*, 252
16. Cooper and Sawaf, *Executive EQ*, xiii
17. Buckingham and Coffman, *First, Break All the Rules*, 252
18. Buckingham and Coffman, *First, Break All the Rules*, 251,252
19. Buckingham and Clifton, *Now Discover Your Strengths*, 78
20. Buckingham and Clifton, *Now Discover Your Strengths*, 78,79
21. Buckingham and Clifton, *Now Discover Your Strengths*, 90
22. Buckingham and Clifton, *Now Discover Your Strengths*, 90
23. Buckingham and Clifton, *Now Discover Your Strengths*, 76

24. Buckingham and Clifton, *Now Discover Your Strengths*, 75,76

Chapter 5 Discipline

1. Michael Treacy and Fred Wiersema, *The Discipline of Market Leaders* (Cambridge, MA: Perseus Books,1997) xi
2. Treacy and Wiersema, *The Discipline of Market Leaders*, xiii
3. Treacy and Wiersema, *The Discipline of Market Leaders*, 31
4. Treacy and Wiersema, *The Discipline of Market Leaders*, 146
5. Treacy and Wiersema, *The Discipline of Market Leaders*, xii
6. Treacy and Wiersema, *The Discipline of Market Leaders*, xii
7. Treacy and Wiersema, *The Discipline of Market Leaders*, 60
8. Treacy and Wiersema, *The Discipline of Market Leaders*, 60
9. Treacy and Wiersema, *The Discipline of Market Leaders*, 60
10. Cooper and Sawaf, *Executive EQ*, xiii
11. Cooper and Sawaf, *Executive EQ*, 42

Chapter 6 Communication

1. Kofman, *Conscious Business*, 245
2. Kofman, *Conscious Business*, 246
3. Cooper and Sawaf, *Executive EQ*, 51
4. Don Miguel Ruiz, The Four Agreements (San Rafael, CA: Amber-Allen Publishing, 1997)

Chapter 7 The Beginning at the End

1. Cooper and Sawaf, *Executive EQ*, xiii

Bibliography

Brewer, Geoffrey and Barb Sanford, eds. *Decade of Change.* New York: Gallup Press, 2011.

Buckingham, Marcus and Donald O. Clifton. *Now, Discover Your Strengths.* New York: The Free Press, 2001.

Buckingham, Marcus and Curt Coffman. *First, Break All the Rules.* New York: Simon and Schuster, 1999.

Collins, Jim. *Good to Great.* New York: Harper Collins, 2001.

Colvin, Geoff. *"Humans are Underrated"* Fortune.com, July 23,2015.

Cooper, Robert K. Ph.D. and Ayman Sawaf, *Executive EQ.* New York: Grosset/Putnam, 1997.

Kofman, Fred. *Conscious Business.* Boulder, Colorado: Sounds True, 2013.

Ruiz, Don Miguel. *The Four Agreements.* San Rafael, California: Amber-Allen Publishing, 1997

Treacy, Michael and Fred Wiersema. *The Discipline of Market Leaders.* Cambridge, Massachusetts: Perseus Books, 1997.

Zakaria, Fareed. *The Post American World.* New York: W.W. Norton And Company, 2008.

Printed in the United States
By Bookmasters